Tales
of a
Barristers' Clerk

Tales
of a
Barristers' Clerk

STEPHEN WARD
and the late
FRANK PARSLIFFE

THE CHOIR PRESS

First published in the United Kingdom in 2020 by
The Choir Press

ISBN 978-1-78963-104-3

To respect the privacy of the barristers, clerks, court staff, lay clients and solicitors we have worked with over the years we have changed some of the details in this book. The dates are random, and the stories go back over a long period of time. Some of the great characters mentioned in this book have sadly passed away but they will always be remembered as generous people who gave time, patience and experience to new junior clerks.

DEDICATION

This book is dedicated to my long-suffering wife Claire. We met in a nightclub in East Grinstead when I was 18, we were engaged when I was 20 and we were married when I was 21. It has been said that behind every successful man is a strong woman and that is certainly true with us. Throughout our marriage of 30 years now, Claire has put up with calls from Barristers all hours of the day and night, weekends and even Christmas Day on one occasion. There have been many trips away, lots of travel, numerous late nights, dinner in the oven, but never a complaint. The life of a Barristers' clerk's wife is not an easy one.

Thank you Claire, love you.

Preface

If you have bought this book, firstly thank you, then secondly, you can be pleased with yourself as you have made a donation directly to the Barristers' Clerks Benevolent Fund. When I set out to write this book I assigned all the royalties to the Benevolent Fund to help clerks or their families who have fallen on hard times. All royalties will go directly from the publishers to the Benevolent Fund. Thank you.

I wanted to write this book because every clerk has a story to tell, every clerk says they will write a book one day, but they don't, or at least very few do. So, I decided to write the book and not leave it until I retire.

This book is about my life as a clerk, it includes stories passed onto me by other clerks working in chambers and, where needed, the identities of those involved have been removed. Some of the stories I have heard over the years may or may not be true, but I never let the truth spoil a good story.

The book is intended to be funny, serious, and share with you a little bit of chambers' life, as I am often asked about the strange world of being a barristers' clerk. Where the terminology is specific to the legal world, I will do my best to explain what it means.

Acknowledgements

Thank you to our contributors:

Martin Poulter

Ben Trott

Martin Secrett

Tim Markham

David Goddard

Philip Alden

Tony Stephenson

Contents

Part One – Tales from the Temple   1

Chapter One   Starting out   3
Chapter Two   Who's who in the law?   24
Chapter Three   How it works   39
Chapter Four   Life in chambers   45
Chapter Five   You have to laugh   67

Part Two – Propping up the bar   95

Chapter One   It all started with Adam   97
Chapter Two   Tom, Dick or Harry   109
Chapter Three   The balloon goes up   124
Chapter Four   Clerks room capers   133
Chapter Five   I become a minder   139
Chapter Six   Tom goes to war   149
Chapter Seven   They also serve who only stand and wait   158
Chapter Eight   A rude awakening   169
Chapter Nine   Now you see it – Now you don't   177

A change of course ...

My story starts as a 16-year-old boy attending my interview at 2 Crown Office Row, 2nd floor, right, in the Temple, London, just off Fleet Street. Most people have no idea that the Temple or the other Inns of Court exist or that they are public places which you can visit any time. If you walk along Fleet Street or the Strand, the Temple is between Fleet Street and the Thames. Walk in, have a look around, it is free and a magical place, often used for film sets. Temple church in particular is worth a visit.

Anyway, I went to 2 COR (as we call it), was introduced to Tom Parsliffe, a large, cheery man who seemed to find everything amusing. Tom was the senior clerk; he was the first clerk I ever met, and I worked with him for some time. Many of the stories in this book involve him, who I will always remember fondly.

This book started as a collection of short stories and then something strange happened which changed the book before it had really begun and here is why.

I received an email from a lady called Claire Long saying her dad Frank had written a book but sadly passed away before it was published. A few email exchanges and a phone call later, I realised that Frank, also known as Tom, was the Tom Parsliffe I had known, so I was surprised to hear he had written his story and that it was about life in chambers long before I arrived.

"1st November 2018

Dear Stephen

Vincent Denham suggested I get in touch with you. I met him at the Chambers UK launch last night and I was telling him how my father [Frank Parsliffe (aka Tom)] worked as a senior clerk in the Temple for 50 years from pre-war to the early 1980s. He had started to write a book about his time in the Temple which was sadly never finished. Vincent had said you were looking for clerk stories for a new publication.

I wondered if you might be interested in what my father had written. He died two years ago but we still have his manuscript, which particularly documents life during the war years in the Temple.

Kind regards,

Claire Long"

I was intrigued and so this book has changed course and is now also a tribute to the late Tom (Frank) Parsliffe. I tell my story including tales from other clerks and then hand over the book to the late Tom who finally gets his story into print and gives you an insight into what clerking was like during and before the war. I hope you enjoy both our stories. Special thanks to Tom's wife Angela and his daughter Claire for allowing me to use his text in this book.

I have been a barristers' clerk in chambers[1] for almost 34 years, working my way from "The Boy"[2] in Middle Temple, to Third Junior in Serjeants Inn, Second Junior in Grays' Inn, then a short spell in

---

[1] Chambers is the terminology for a collection of barristers. The Oxford English Dictionary says the word chambers is a collection of rooms, commonly occupied by barristers.

[2] The Boy is the term used for a new, starter clerk, fresh from school. The boy does everything from pushing trolleys laden with papers from court to making tea, running to the shop, buying sandwiches to answering the phone and speaking to solicitors.

Manchester as a Junior before settling in Somerset in 1993 when I became a Senior Clerk, the most senior position you can achieve in the clerking world. Aged 21, it was a steep learning curve as nobody ever tells you what a senior clerk does. It is a complete mystery to most junior clerks.

These stories are historical and in recent years more formal training and dedicated courses have been developed to teach modern business skills to new clerks which is a great advancement.

The route taken by a youngster wanting to be a barristers' clerk begins as The Boy, progressing to Third Junior, Second Junior, Junior and finally Senior Clerk. Generally speaking, each stage is reached by moving to another set of chambers.

PART ONE
Tales from the Temple

Stephen Ward

CHAPTER ONE
Starting out

How did you become a barristers' clerk?

This is one of the most frequently asked questions at dinner parties, social events and on camp sites. Most clerks will have a story to tell about how they first got into clerking as it such a strange world and not generally understood by those outside of the profession.

For me I was 15 and a half. I had been quite naughty at school and never really had much interest in learning. I just wanted to earn some money and spend it. By 14, I had become quite good at both and had my own successful lawn mowing business with friends helping out. My dad had loaned me the money to buy a petrol Flymo from a catalogue and then a petrol strimmer. I was too young to drive so we re-engineered a set of old pram wheels to take the Flymo, strimmer, broom and edging shears.

I lived just outside Brighton in a place called Telscombe Cliffs. The roads are ordered in a grid formation so we would work our way up one road and back down the other side one day, then the next road the next and so on. All after school or weekends. Sometimes during school times, but only when mum and dad were away, which resulted in me getting to know the headmaster quite well and the chair outside his office, which was plastic from memory and quite uncomfortable.

I recall coming home in the evening for dinner, placing a large amount of cash on the table and working out what percentage was right to pay my mum for housekeeping, which was always the deal in our house. Mum used to tell us that when we earn, we pay our way which was fair.

Anyway, I had a passion for business, working and earning. My school finally gave up on me at Easter when I was 15+ years while others undertook what I think they called study leave for O Levels. I had no need to study as I clearly knew everything. Of course, I was wrong, and my parents and teachers were right, but it is now too late. I do however acknowledge it. Whenever anyone asked my parents what I was likely to be doing when I was older they would shrug with despair and say either he is going to be a millionaire or he will be in prison ... I have not achieved either as yet!

So, there I was aged 15 with the likelihood I would have no qualifications at all and had pretty much left school. I needed to go back for exams but that was just a formality. I did actually get an O Level in Geography because I enjoyed that subject and also a good result in Technical Drawing as the teacher was stunning and I always attended her classes. She used to lean over the desk from the other side to help and she always wore low cut blouses. It kept me interested in Technical Drawing and I always had lots of questions for her!

Then my dad asked me the dreaded question, "What are you going to do?" Quite frankly I had no idea as the lawn mowing was easy money but not really a career I saw myself doing unless all else failed. So, I started to look for a proper job with an employer and was soon offered a job doing general labouring on a building site.

Within a few weeks, the owner took me aside and asked if I would take responsibility for the site and handed me the keys. He said, "You are always in early, the last to leave and you take pride in what you do. I want you to watch over the site to make sure people are here when they say there are and things don't go missing". I held that position of trust until the day I left.

One day while locking up, the owner invited me into his house to meet his wife and have a drink. He was complimentary about me and asked if I would like to become a barristers' clerk. I asked him what a barristers' clerk was and he explained, "You will need to go to London and work in the Temple."[3]

---

[3]   Temple is an area of London between the Strand and the Embankment. The area was given to the Inns of Court when Lawyers were banned from the City. The area known as Temple was just outside Ludgate Circus, the gateway to the City of London. In the 14th century lawyers were excluded from practising within the City of London limits. The land was given to lawyers for them to practice and for education. This land must be handed back to the Crown if it is

That evening I explained to my parents what had happened, particularly about the "Temple" as they had always warned me about religious people trying to brainwash you and told me to beware. I never thought that it would ever happen to me so when I told my parents about this I felt immensely proud that my parents had warned me of these things and that I had listened to them. My dad replied with, "It is a place In London where Barristers work, stupid boy".

The next day on site when the owner returned at the end of the day, I asked more about the role which he explained as, "You need to work hard, do what you are told and don't reply. And by the way, you call ladies Ma'am and men Sir." He duly arranged an interview a few days later.

Mum bought me my first suit, a shirt and pink tie (not sure about the pink tie to this day). Photo taken by proud parents seeing their boy in a suit, and off I went to London for my interview.

A bus to Brighton which was six miles away, a short walk from the bus stop to the station, a train to London, a tube from Victoria to Temple and a short walk to 2 Crown Office Row. There I met Jean Brett, the lady in charge of the Institute of Barristers' Clerks Association who told me to just answer honestly and I would be alright. Interview coaching out the way, I was introduced to Tom Parsliffe, the Senior Clerk.

He was puffing on a cigarette, had an ancient typewriter on his desk, which was piled high with papers tied up with pink ribbon. He told me he was taking me to see Mr Arthur Mildon Q.C. who would interview me.

A few minutes later and I was sitting in front of the 'Head of Chambers', Arthur Mildon Q.C. I was very nervous before but now I

---

ever not used for this purpose, so the Inns continue to thrive as the main London home for Barristers in England and Wales. Today there are four Inns of court – Lincolns' Inn, Gray's Inn, Middle Temple and Inner Temple. See Wikipedia for Inns of Court and the history.

think even 'terrified' might well be an understatement. He was reading some papers and so I sat quietly until he glanced up. He looked me up and down and asked what football team I supported to which I replied, "I'm not really into football".

"Umph," came from him. However, he thanked me for my time and I was shown the door. Tom laughed again, took me back to the Clerks' Room, asked me a few questions, thanked me for coming and said they would be in touch and I left.

Somewhat bemused I did the return journey home by tube, train, bus and walking. As I walked up to the front door I found my excited dad waiting on the doorstep. He said, "I've just had a phone call from Arthur Mildon Q.C. and he says make sure you are in by 9am tomorrow to start your new job" (and of course I was).

As it turned out, the chap who owned the building site worked at the Director of Public Prosecutions[4] at Queen Anne's Gate and had already spoken to Arthur Mildon Q.C. at court, explained about me and my work ethic, told him how much he trusted me and put in a good word. So even failing the football test, I still passed and all he wanted to check was that I didn't have two heads.

I went straight round to see the building site owner to thank him and to this day I remain eternally grateful. Martin Woodnut was his name, a name I will never forget.

The next morning I suited up, left home at 6.30am, caught the bus, train, tube and appeared at 2 Crown Office Row. Tom sat at his type-writer to type out, Tippex correct, re-type, Tippex out again and then redo my contract.

---

[4]   The Director of Public Prosecutions (DPP) is the office charged with the prosecution of criminal offences in several criminal jurisdictions around the world.

Telephone: (01) 583 8155
Telex: 886010 CORLAW
L.D.E. Box No. 1041

2 CROWN OFFICE ROW,
THE TEMPLE,
LONDON EC4Y 7HJ

June 21st, 1985

Dear Stephen,

I am writing to set out the proposed terms
of employment which I offer on behalf of Mr. Arthur
Mildon Q.C., as head of these Chambers :

(i) You will commence employment on Monday, 24th June
1985, and be subject to one months's trial period.
If, at the end of one full month's employment both sides
feel that the trial has been satisfactory, a further
period of two months' trial will be entered into,
a#the end of which time (I.E. 3 full months' employment)
a final decision will be made regarding the offer of
a permanent position with us.

(2) The annual salary will be £3,000 (which will
include travelling expenses).

(3) Starting time in the mornings will be 9 a.m. but
every attempt will be made to release you in the
evenings, if possible, before 5.30   p.m.

(6)   Other details (such as lunch times) can be

negotiated in due course.

I trust that you may find the above terms
acceptable and that, if you join us, you will be happy
working with us.

Yours sincerely,

F.B. PARSLIFFE
Clerk to Chambers.

Void as from 5/March/86.

My salary stated in the contract was £3,000 a year. Wow, I was in the money.

With the help of a loan from the bank of Mum and Dad, I bought a
weekly pass for the bus, the train and the tube – £41 a week, I remember
it very clearly. Take home pay slip, £52.49 (I still have every one of them
in my loft). 6.30am to 8pm five days a week, working flat out for £11.49.
I soon realised I was not in the money after all and dreamt of lawn
mowing.

On one day I remember calling my dad from a payphone[5] in my
lunchtime as I was in tears because the barristers had been so unkind to
me and my dad said, "Don't you dare chuck it all in, you have no choice

---

[5]   A Payphone was something that was in the UK before mobile phones came along. They
were small red boxes dotted around the streets with a telephone that you put coins into
and could speak to someone on their phone.

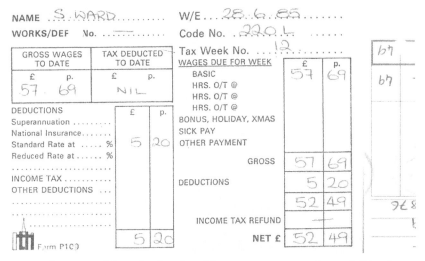

remember, you skipped school and have no exam results to fall back on. Get on with it". His sympathetic words made it all good again and I did just get on with it.

To this day I never understand why Barristers are rude to clerks as it always seems to me they would get a better service from any human being if they were nice and asked politely. Anyway, my career began and I was officially "The Boy".

Sir and Ma'am

When I began as a junior clerk at 2 Crown Office Row in the Temple, London, male barristers were called Sir and female barristers were Ma'am. I remember to this day when I moved to 3 Serjeants Inn and was told I could not speak to barristers by their surnames. I was 16 so it was 1985. I recall clearly the first barrister I called by their name was Miss Powell. It was a big deal for me at the time and did feel very strange.

Is a barrister's clerk training to be a lawyer?

No, barristers' clerks train to be senior clerks, dealing only with administration and practice development. Solicitors' clerks train to be solicitors. The two professions are strangely different.

History of the barristers' clerk

Barristers' clerk or Clerk to Counsel. The word 'clerk' gives most people the wrong impression of the role. It suggests a subordinate employee in an office.

Barristers' clerks are divided into junior and senior clerks. Junior clerks progress to become senior clerks if they work hard enough (some say trial by ordeal!), and keep their noses clean.

There are about 400 senior clerks in the UK and a total of 3,000 barristers' clerks. Barristers' clerks learn their trade by working on the job and learning about the legal profession by gaining experience from more senior clerks. I became a senior clerk in 1993 – at the time aged 25 years I was the youngest senior clerk in the UK.

What is the difference between a barrister and a solicitor?

I am often asked the question: "What is the difference between a barrister and a solicitor?"

Solicitors have traditionally been the first port of call for those seeking general legal advice, however that is now changing with the introduction of the public access rules for Barristers. The Law Society is the professional body who represents solicitors.

I often liken it to a GP and consultant. If you have a general medical issue you see your GP who will refer you onto a specialist if they think it is more complex. The same is true for a solicitor who will refer a legal issue to a barrister either for a hearing or settling some paperwork (pleadings[6]) but also if the issue is complex or they simply want a more experienced lawyer to give them another view.

---

[6] Pleadings In law as practiced in countries that follow the English models, these are a formal written statement of a party's claims or defences to another party's claims in a civil action. The parties' pleadings in a case define the issues to be adjudicated in the action. The Civil Procedure Rules (CPR) govern pleadings in England and Wales.

9

Barristers, on the other hand, have not traditionally dealt with members of the public directly, but take their instructions from a solicitor who is representing the client. Barristers then represent the client at court and present their case. The Bar Council is the professional body who represents barristers.

To-do list for the junior clerk

One day, my then senior clerk Nick Salt at 3 Serjeants Inn, handed me a huge list of tasks and said simply: "can you do these today please?" I looked at the list and was completely baffled, there was about a month's work, all set out in a neat and tidy schedule.

Nick liked lists. I sat at my desk for about 15 minutes looking at the list and summoned up the courage to go back to the senior clerk and ask what the priority was as it was not possible to do everything that day. A rather confused Nick look at me and explained I just needed to do what was on the list and that was that. Still worried I explained the list was far too long and it simply would not be possible. Then Nick explained it was

Nick Salt in formal attire

only the highlighted items in pink I needed to do to which I replied: "But there are no items highlighted". It was at that point I realised my colour blindness meant I could not see a pink highlighter on white paper and it all became clear.

Nick changed the task list to yellow highlights and the few items on the list designated to me were completed that day.

My personal I.T. journey

My personal I.T. journey started 35-years ago. I was 16 and I joined 2 Crown Office Row in the Temple, London as 'The Boy', a title given to the most junior clerk in chambers (the title applied at the time, even if the boy was a lady). Male barristers were called Sir and female Barristers Ma'am.

I was given the job by the then Senior Clerk, Tom Parsliffe (RIP) who typed out my offer letter and contract on his typewriter in front of me, then covered half the page with Tippex, re-typed it and the resulting mess became my first ever contract of employment. I've held onto that letter to this day as I couldn't believe that the legal world I was about to enter, full of all its formalities, would present me with such a document. I've come to love that letter and contract over the years because it demonstrates quite clearly what life was like then and how far we have come. My salary, clearly set out (the only part not covered in Tippex) was £52.49 a week. This was paid weekly in cash, in a small brown envelope.

We had no computers then, no faxes and no mobile phones. We had a paper diary that we had to have made each year and was on a huge metal contraption which swung round so all the clerks could view this huge, hand-made diary with sections for all the barristers' names on a single view, per day. Queen's Counsel at the top, juniors descending in call order. The diary never swivelled much, it always stayed in front of Tom, the senior clerk, as he was in total control of the clerking team and the barristers. I cannot comment about pupils, I hardly ever saw them, other than in the tea room, as they were banned from the clerks room.

It was 1984, the year George Orwell predicted that Great Britain would be called 'Airstrip One' and would be a province of a super state named Oceania. He predicted all this in 1949. While his book was a work of literary political fiction, he still predicted such things as 'Big Brother', 'Newspeak' and the 'manipulation of recorded history'. Sadly George died in 1950 aged only 46 but I wonder what people must have thought about his predictions back then. I suspect most people thought he was simply bonkers.

I thought about this a lot as I pushed my trolley up and down Fleet Street, the Strand, Aldwych and Chancery Lane. I spent about one hour each afternoon of my working life at that time visiting the basement of the Royal Courts of Justice where the listing room was located. All the clerks used to meet there, it was like a Facebook group of listing clerks, all very sociable. Come to think of it, we never mentioned what we had for lunch, or took in a Polaroid of a cat pulling a funny face. We seemed to be happy despite that. I cannot recall what we talked about.

Today, in 2020, the world of Legal I.T. is all about robot lawyers taking over the world, blockchain, artificial intelligence, analytics and research, law for good, digitisation of the court service, contract analysis and big data for checking the complexities of acquisitions and mergers.

There is very little talk about innovation in case management systems for solicitors or barristers. I know there is a lot of hard work going on out there by the software companies and the passionate individuals who work for them, but it is often overlooked as it is not considered to be sexy so not newsworthy.

In 1985, I was asked by Nick Salt, the senior clerk at 3 Serjeants Inn, if I wanted to move from 2COR and help set up the new ACE chambers computer system. I agreed. We were going to take all the A5 cards from the cabinet in the corner of the clerks room and input them into the computer. We had to carefully remove all the coloured tags from the corner of the cards, the A4 folded copies of letters and type them individually into this new box. It hardly seemed big enough as there were a lot of cards. The chambers computer was about the size of six large Pizza boxes stacked one on top of the other and then there was a very large green screen that had a white flashing dot in the bottom left corner which became visible about 15 minutes after you pressed the on button at the front.

I was fascinated by this box and all that it could do. I was 17, I was a mini entrepreneur, after all I had already run my own lawn mowing business since the age of 14 with staff and contracts for holiday parks and blocks of flats. I realised the very first day I saw this 'computer' it could do some of the tasks that we had previously had to pay staff to do and therefore there could be a significant cost saving and make us all more efficient. I could see no way of this box helping to mow lawns so I ended that business, pushed my trolley up and down Chancery Lane to the DX and began to think about what computers could do for the world of law.

How could a computer collect the DX, make the tea for barristers, pick up food from the sandwich shops, order taxis to take barristers to court, finally do away with the travel agency books we used to have in chambers to write out our own train tickets for barristers. Clearly computers would not replace us, it cannot do these tasks, it would simply help us and make the clerk's life a breeze. It seemed that this magic box was going to change the way we all worked and I was right there, at the very start of it all.

My second year as a barristers' clerk and I was sitting in front of the magic box with its big screen and huge printer that took the place of the old filing cabinet in the corner. Life was very exciting. (Remember, this was pre-Facebook.)

Skip forward 10 years as I cannot remember much of what happened between 1985 and 1995 other than I got married, moved chambers, had kids, became a senior clerk and the original chambers computer company had been bought out by a larger software company (who used to provide software for bus companies so they could predict when buses would need maintenance and get them to the right place at the right time with the right outcomes. It seemed to me that had a lot of similarities to barristers' and chambers' diaries).

So it is 1995, chambers has a bigger box called a server, same size screen and back up tapes. We had to sit and wait for the tapes to finish recording the day's work and most nights we just sat and waved goodbye to the barristers who said they would meet us in the pub when the tapes had finished and we had delivered them to the off-site storage half a mile away. But by this point, we had a 'network', a way of connecting our boxes and screens together so we could save the chambers information into one place. But we still had a big red purpose designed diary as it was decided we could never trust the computer to hold the diary information. The diary is the 'bible' in most chambers.

In Scotland, the diaries for each barrister are still located in the law library in Edinburgh as they always have been. There is now a project to move them onto a computer system but that is ongoing. (In 2003, I was asked to do some consultancy work for the Faculty of Advocates in Edinburgh, so I spent some time working with them in the law library and with faculty services. I prepared a report called 'Modernisation of the Scottish Faculty of Advocates Clerking Service' which I understand is now being prepared to be rolled out.)

In 1997 the members of chambers, the management committee, the head of chambers and the treasurer all made the momentous decision to allow the clerks to load the chambers diary onto the computer system. This was a massive step for chambers and me as senior clerk. What if it went wrong? Anyway, it didn't go wrong, it just made life easier and I could view the barristers' diaries out of chambers hours, in the evenings, weekends and while I was on holiday, that made it so much better for them.

Please bear in mind that we used ISDN (Integrated Services Digital Network) in those days as the Internet was invented but was used as a miltary asset. ISDN allowed us to 'dial in' to the chambers server via a loud and screechy modem and once (if) connected, allowed us to view the diary on the chambers' server. Quite frankly, this was remarkable and mind blowing at the time, but expensive.

A quick history lesson and a few big facts, – everyone loves big stats:

Two years before this, in August 1995, a completely unknown chap called Bill Gates, who lived in an equally unknown place in America called Silicon Valley, came up with a computer program that would make it easier for anyone to operate a computer and he called it 'Windows 95'. Bill was really busy because in December that year he also came up with Internet Explorer (I.E.1.0) which it was claimed would make using the Internet much easier. Even better, they would integrate this new Internet Explorer into Windows 95 so it made life simply brilliant for all Windows 95 computer users.

By the end of 1995, various tech products were emerging from America but nothing was uniform or mainstream. The Internet reached a third of all US households by mid-1999 and 50% by 2001. In 2018, the number of Internet users in the world passed the four billion mark, which means that well over half of the world's population is now online, with the latest data showing that nearly a quarter of a billion new users came online for the first time in 2017.

Growth in Africa is at 20% year on year. Much of the worldwide growth continues due to the use of smart phones as data plans have become more affordable. Now for some big numbers!

1. 200 million people got their first mobile device in 2017
2. Two-thirds of the world's 7.6 billion inhabitants now have a mobile phone
3. More than half of the handsets in use today are 'smart' devices
4. 3 billion people around the world now use social media every month
5. 9 out of 10 social media users access their chosen platforms via a mobile device
6. The global number of internet users in 2018 was 4.021 billion, up 7% on the previous year
7. The number of social media users in 2018 was 3.196 billion, up 13% on the previous year

8. The number of mobile phone users in 2018 was 5.135 billion, up 4% on the previous year.

9. If you add together all 4 billion internet users, all spending time on the internet, it is a staggering total of 1 billion years of time spent online in 2018 alone

Back in the room: It is now 1998, BT offer Internet to our homes and I can change my ISDN line at home for Internet at a fixed, low cost. _This got me thinking!_ If we could connect our houses to the Internet for a fixed, low monthly cost, the barristers could work easily from home and not in chambers every day.

Of course this was all about saving chambers rent for office space, nothing to do with my 30 barristers all coming into chambers each day, saying good morning, having a jolly chat about what they had been up to since I saw them at 5pm yesterday, asking me if I'd had time to issue a claim form to the Crown Court, chased solicitors for the next day's papers, completed all the marketing tasks they had kindly provided me with, prepared the reports for the chambers meeting that night at 8pm. We repeated this again when they passed though the clerks room on the way to have lunch with each other, chambers solicitor clients, wives and partners, all of course stopping to ask the clerking team why they had not managed to issue that urgent fee note or move a court hearing as they now wanted to go on holiday that week. The clerks would work through lunch with a sandwich at the desk as we could actually get some work done while they were out. Then we repeat the process above but in reverse order as our members arrive back from a nice lunch and entertaining. Some became slightly more aggressive and assertive after lunch and now demanded that the fees were issued, collected and paid into their banks by close of play that day, all perfectly reasonable of course, it is what clerks do. Remember, it was 1998, things were like that then, we just got on with it. I have no grudges, honest.

The Internet years and our journey:

1. 1993 Chambers agreed to a publish a website
2. 1999 Chambers updated the website and we offered a form to allow enquiries online
3. 2000 Chambers rejected the idea that barristers might work from home
4. 2001 Clerksroom was launched as a nationwide chambers in April with one clerk and two barristers
5. 2002 Clerksroom launch online booking – Clerksroom online
6. 2004 Clerksroom launch Clerksroom Mediation, a nationwide mediation service
7. 2014 Clerksroom launch Clerksroom Direct, the public access portal
8. 2018 Clerksroom launch Billy Bot, the robot junior clerk and chatbot
9. 2019 Clerksroom has 105 Barristers and 23 clerks. Clerksroom.com

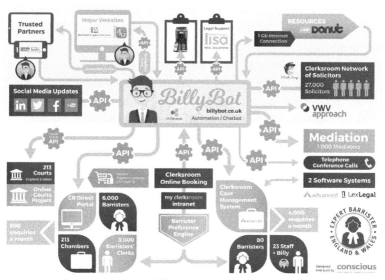

Image to show how Billy Bot works using API technology

Chambers Case Management System

By 2014 it had become clear that the world was quickly heading towards the new Internet savvy client, be it a professional or lay client. Clients can now shop around, find out much more about our services, compare prices and make informed choices about their legal purchase. We had to up our game, it was obvious. But how?

Having undertaken a review of our chambers online and offline systems and processes throughout 2014, we realised we had to build a purpose-built case management system for public access clients as the rules, needs, and software were quite different for a public access case to a traditional instruction that came into chambers. Firstly there was a new frustration that lay clients needed more time on the phone to explain what a barrister can do to help them, regularly between 30 to 60 mins of time per call with a less than 20% conversion rate from enquiry to purchase. This had to stop or it would simply take over the clerks' time and lead to meltdown. So we built our own public access portal in line with the Bar Standards Board rules and regulations to streamline the instruction process, the payment process, the case management process and automate the regulatory issues like money laundering checks, proceeds of crime act checks, identification and so on. All very easy to automate.

Having achieved success with over 6,000 public access clients and our brilliant team of dedicated public access clerks achieving a conversion rate (enquiry to payment) of 54.29%, we realised that we needed to review all our main chambers systems and processes. Not an easy task.

In 2015 and 2016 we started our journey in the world of APIs (application programming interface) having achieved success with the public access case management system. We integrated our online systems with our existing case management system with great help from our supplier at the time and continued to build software that would talk between our web systems and third-party systems.

In early 2017 it became clear that this strategy had no long-term future and we needed to take ownership of the problem we felt we faced. The problem being, how do we keep up with the world at large, our existing and new clients' expectations, the growing need for analytics and restructuring of data into new databases that allowed for online service expansion, visibility and collaboration? Couple this with the new requirements from HMRC where barristers have to make tax digital from 5 April 2019 and the opening up of the banking system in 2019 with the introduction of the OBR rules. We needed to find a way to integrate chambers case management system with the barristers own bookkeeping and expenses systems, allow their bookkeepers access, letting lay and professional clients into our systems to view their case and fee data while making it all GDPR and HMRC compliant and secure. That is before we even start with the basics like marketing and day to day diary management, fee collection and compliance with debt protocols. Now we are obliged to sue solicitors for non-payment of fees in the same way as everyone else does. (We used to have a protocol between the Bar Council and the Law Society where you could report a firm for non-payment but that has sadly ended now and our only option is to sue for unpaid debts in the usual way.)

The answer was to go back to the drawing board and work out what we, as a chambers, needed and then work out how to build it, or even if we could afford it. Every member of our clerking team has been involved in the project and every full-time barrister on our team has been invited to contribute ideas. The resulting 78-page specification covers all the normal aspects of chambers life including:

1. Security and GDPR compliance
2. Fair allocation of work policies (now part of the BSB diversity rules)
3. The software requirements of our barrister members, clients and staff
4. Databases, how to keep them updated and fresh
5. Diary management of 128 diaries
6. Automated invoicing
7. Automated cheque, BACS and payment processing together with credit card payments

8. Expense management and chambers bookkeeping
9. Marketing and integration with common platforms like Mailchimp, linking back to the databases for unsubscribes and updates
10. Document and data storage in a secure, cost effective and easy to use way
11. Mobile connectivity and ease of use
12. Credit control and debt collection protocols
13. Mediation administration
14. Public access administration
15. Chat bot integration
16. Wallboards and analytics
17. Reporting with ease on any question
18. Integration with barristers own bookkeeping software and expenses apps management
19. Complaints handling
20. Diversity monitoring
21. Contractual terms and CFA management

It became clear to us (the management board at Clerksroom) that we needed to approach this from a blank sheet of paper and work out what we needed, what the timescale for the build was and if we could afford it.

So we designed and built www.Chambers365.com with huge assistance from Microsoft and Xero who provided us with all the support we needed throughout. Our designers and developers are morphsites who undertook the migration tasks, delivered the project on time, on budget with no major issues. At peak and critical times morphsites had up to 37 people working on our project to ensure that it was delivered as they said it would be. The project cost was divided into monthly amounts allowing us to pay for the development as we went along and in a very agile way.

What we have now is very much the *starting point of our new journey* into the real world of legal tech. What an exciting time it is to be involved in legal tech. 2019 was fun.

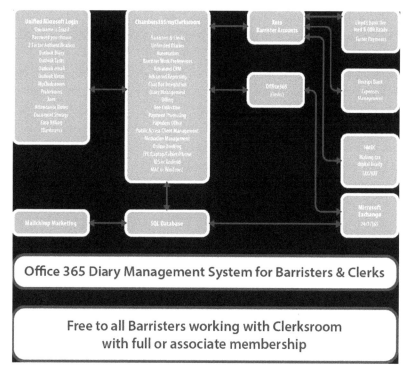

Office 365 Diary Management System for Barristers & Clerks

Free to all Barristers working with Clerksroom with full or associate membership

Acknowledgements:

The Chambers365 project was only possible because of the knowledge, skill and dedication of all the clerking team at Clerksroom, Harry Hodgkin, Head of Chambers, Financial Director, Co-founder and full-time commercial barrister. Our barristers have had to put up with a huge amount of inconvenience as we messed up their I.T., created havoc with emails, documents and changed familiar systems and logins to much frustration. But we are there now, so thank you all.

The life of a barrister's clerk's wife

... is never going to be easy. Late night working, chambers parties, relentless travel, stress and calls all through the night from Barristers making completely unreasonable demands.

Add to that the countless missed key dates like wedding anniversaries, or key times in the lives of our children, like sports days, birthdays being missed. I once had a call from a Barrister on my mobile while I was watching my son at his primary school sports day and told to: "Get back to chambers now," as there was a crisis. When I got back to chambers I was advised it had all been sorted out.

I met Claire when I was 18 and a junior clerk, we married at 21, she gave up her career for me as I moved to Manchester and she has put up with me ever since, almost 30 years now.

I can understand why many Barristers Clerks' marriages break down as work really does (or did) come first and the family came second. These days thankfully employers are a bit wiser to the benefits of a better work life balance and remote working but it is not always been like that and Claire has been supportive every step of the way.

The top 10 people I have worked with and have influenced me the most

1. Nick Salt, the Senior Clerk at 3 Serjeants Inn
2. Robert Allen, the Senior Clerk at Atkin Chambers
3. Terry Creathorn, 1st Junior Clerk at Deans Court Chambers
4. Tom, or was it Frank, Parsliffe, Senior Clerk at 2 Crown Office Row
5. Martin Secrett, 1st Junior Clerk at 2 Crown Office Row
6. Mary Kelsey who interviewed me at South Western Chambers and has stayed working with and helping me to this day
7. Harry Hodgkin, Barrister, Head of Chambers, Finance Director at Clerksroom
8. Martin Davies, Chambers Director at Clerksroom from launch in 2001 until 2018 when a more exciting challenge drew him away
9. Mike Stubbs, Senior Clerk at Parklane Plowden, Newcastle
10. Martin Poulter, Chambers People and now our London office manager too

As a barristers' clerk you meet hundreds, if not thousands of people, in your career and many of them influence the way you work. There are too many to list but you know who you are.

CHAPTER 2

Who's who in the law?

"The barrister's clerk"

Re-printed with the permission of 3 Paper Buildings

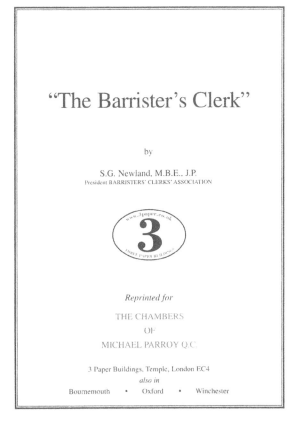

"The Barrister's Clerk"

by

S.G. Newland, M.B.E., J.P.
President BARRISTERS' CLERKS' ASSOCIATION

3
www.3paper.co.uk
THREE PAPER BUILDINGS

Reprinted for

THE CHAMBERS
OF
MICHAEL PARROY Q.C.

3 Paper Buildings, Temple, London EC4
also in
Bournemouth • Oxford • Winchester

FOREWORD

In June 1971 Mr. S.G. Newland the President of our association gave a lecture on *The Barrister's Clerk* to students of the Barristers' Clerks' Association. This lecture was attended not only by students, but also by many other members anxious not to miss an opportunity of listening to him.

What follows is a record of that lecture reproduced not only for Barristers' Clerks, but also for all who are interested in the Legal Profession.

Before becoming President of the Association, Mr Newland was Chairman for over 30 years. He is a former Mayor of Wembley, a Justice of the Peace, and was awarded the M.B.E. in 1968.

It is indeed for me both a pleasure and a privilege to introduce this lecture.

CYRIL BATCHELOR
Chairman of the Barristers' Clerks' Association

It is my privilege to endeavour to give to you a thumbnail sketch of what you have chosen to become, namely a barrister's clerk or, as I prefer to put it, 'Clerk to Counsel.' The word 'clerk' immediately conjures up a picture of a subordinate employee in an office, keeping records, assisting in correspondence – tied to a desk. That is an almost completely untrue picture of a barrister's senior clerk. The word is also applied to another group of people whose tasks are far more exacting and onerous, such as Clerks of the Peace, Clerks to the Justices, Clerks to County Councils and Surveyors who are Clerks of Works, to give only a few examples. and I believe we belong in that group under the appellation of 'Clerk to Counsel.'

I think this is important not from a snobbish point of view, but because I think that from the outset you should be made aware of the responsible nature of your position, and also that those with whom we have to deal should not be misled into thinking that some inferior servant has been deputed to the task of dealing with their affairs.

From time immemorial counsel of the English Bar have had attached to them a clerk. There are probably more today than there have ever been before, but even now there are only about 240 senior clerks in the whole of England and Wales. Never before has any one of them been asked to attend a course of lectures to qualify for membership of our Association or to pass a subsequent examination and, in addition, to have an educational qualification.

Does this mean then that hitherto we have been creatures of ignorance? Indeed it does not. It means that when we started in chambers, although generally speaking we had no special skills, we ultimately gained a thorough knowledge of our duties by actual experience from day to day. Those who had not got the ability to learn or the aptitude, sooner or later fell by the wayside. Those who survived and found themselves selected as senior clerks had had the additional advantage of being thrown into daily constant contact with members of the Bar, men and women of erudition and ability whose professional conduct is at the highest possible level. What better University could a barrister's clerk have or desire?

Those of us, therefore, who have succeeded have been tried by ordeal far more discerning than any examination at the outset of our career could possibly have been. But the present is an age where there is almost a craze for dividing people into those who have qualified and those who have not. Your Association has decided, therefore, to institute a method of qualification in order to encourage recruitment. Whether the finished product will be any better remains to be seen; but on the face of it the raising of the standard of entry may mean that not so many will fall by the wayside and the pooling of knowledge of methods and organisation should raise the level of administration. The work that has been put into this series of lectures is stupendous and the Senior Lecturer, Stanley Turner, and all his assistants deserve the greatest possible thanks.

Many extremely interesting books have been written about the four Inns of Court and I would recommend every young man who wants to become a clerk to counsel to study at least one of them.

The Temple in the twelfth century was owned by the Knights Templars. The Round Church was built by them in 1185. When they fell into disfavour in the early fourteenth century their property was eventually given by the Crown to the Order of St John. but as these gentlemen already had a vast estate at Clerkenwell they let it out to the people who taught, learnt and practised law, who about this time had been excluded from the City of London by a writ of King Henry III. They flourished, formed themselves into societies, which they called Inns of Court. and somehow acquired the exclusive right to grant the right of audience, that is the right to practise in the courts, to their members.

There were different kinds of lawyers, some were better speakers than others and specialised in advocacy and others studied more deeply the knowledge of law. Today your practising lawyers are broadly divided into two branches: the barristers and the solicitors. The barristers are members of one of the four remaining Inns of Court, namely Lincoln's Inn. the Inner Temple, the Middle Temple and Gray's Inn, and most solicitors are members of the Law Society.

How can I best describe in a few sentences the difference between the work of the two branches? The ordinary man in the street, the lay client, who feels he has been wronged, or wants to take some legal step or be advised, must first go to a solicitor, like the sick man who goes to a general practitioner, a doctor. The solicitor may say to him; 'this is a simple matter' and deals with the matter for him; or he may say 'this is a complicated matter, we must go to a specialist', a barrister who specialises in this branch of the law or who specialises in advocacy or has the right of audience in higher courts. The lay client cannot go direct to the barrister; he must first go to the solicitor. You have decided to throw in your lot with the barristers.

When the lawyers originally took over the Temple from the Knights Templars they used to live as well as work in chambers, and so did their clerks. We have a most interesting record of this fact at a much later period, namely about 1775, because in that year at No.2, Crown Office Row, was born Charles Lamb who is acknowledged to have been one of the most brilliant essayists of English literature. He was the son of John Lamb who was clerk to Mr. Salt, K.C., a Bencher of the Inner Temple, and lived in rooms attached to his chambers. We can read in one of Charles Lamb's essays called 'The Old Benchers of the Inner Temple' a description of his father's relationship with his principal, which is fascinatingly true of such relationships today and we can learn much from a study of it.

He wrote, about his father: 'He was at once his clerk, his good servant, dresser, his friend, his flapper, his guide, stop watch, auditor, treasurer. He did nothing without consulting him, or failed in anything without expecting and fearing his admonishing. He resigned his title almost to respect as a master, if his clerk could ever have forgotten for a moment that he was his servant.'

John Lamb had been sent up from the country as a youngster to go into the service of Mr. Salt and, like many hundreds of other clerks to counsel. he grew up to be absolutely indispensable to his Principal. Even in those days for every guinea that Mr. Salt was paid by the client, the client in addition paid to John Lamb five percent as a clerk's fee, and this clerk's fee is in force to this day; the only difference being that up to a month or so ago it was chargeable in addition to the fee agreed for counsel but now one composite fee is agreed which includes counsel's fee and clerk's fee.

When the Principal became too busy he would take into his chambers other barristers to do some of his work and the clerk would act as clerk to them as well. They would not be taken in as partners because, as you will learn in the lectures on etiquette, barristers are not allowed to have partners. They share their rooms, they share their books, they share their clerk, but sometimes they are on opposite sides in the same case so they could not possibly be partners.

Talking of helping with the work reminds me that there is a well-known term in use which is called 'devilling.' It refers to the occasions when counsel is so busy that he gets a less busy member of the Bar to help him with his work. If the help is given in court, the permission of the instructing solicitor ought always to be obtained. Round about 1760 there used to be a little tavern just outside the Middle Temple gate and if counsel suddenly found he was wanted in two courts at the same time he or his clerk would rush into this tavern, get hold of some drunken barrister and hurriedly enlist his services in one of the courts. This was called 'devilling.' The name of the tavern was 'The Devil' and you can see a commemorative plaque on the wall of Child's Bank, No. I, Fleet Street, marking the spot.

The tendency nowadays is for sets of chambers to grow larger and instead of one Mr. Salt there are sometimes twenty or thirty barristers sharing the same clerk, but basically the duties of the clerk remain the same.

What are they? What makes a good clerk?

Let us remember from the outset never to forget for a moment that we are all the servant or agent. A rude or surly or overbearing clerk does our profession a great disservice and does himself no good. When I first came into the Temple almost every senior clerk wore a morning coat and many of them wore silk hats.

I am not going to suggest that you should go back to those days but our habit and bearing should be such as to command respect. for it will be difficult for us to carry out our duties if we are not taken seriously. One of the greatest attributes of counsel is his diction. We clerks should emulate them. Many of us were born Cockneys, but it is not necessary to thrust this fact down everybody's ears.

We act as a go-between between the instructing solicitor and counsel. One of our main duties is to arrange with the instructing solicitor what fee should be paid to our Principal for a particular task. In this respect the responsibility that is yours is to see that a *proper* fee is arranged. In arriving at a proper fee you should take into consideration first the weight and complexity of the work to be done; secondly. the standing and ability of the counsel concerned and then, thirdly, you have the task of considering, if required, the ability of the client to pay a proper fee. A clerk who demands unfair fees soon loses his goodwill with solicitors – in effect he prices himself out of the market – and when, as often is the case, a solicitor says: 'I must leave you to charge what is proper, because he has no experience of what is a proper fee, you must be meticulously careful not to violate that trust, and always remember that although you undoubtedly have a duty to see that your Principal is properly remunerated, you owe a duty to the lay client to see that he is not fleeced.

It is sometimes said that the fact that the clerk's remuneration is tied to that of his Principal results in the clerk pushing up the fee. One thing on which all experienced clerks agree is that during the negoti- ation of a fee that factor never obtrudes on their thoughts. Don't ever let it. You will learn other things with regard to the fixing of fees under the lecture on etiquette.

Having accepted a brief from a solicitor for one of your Principals, it is your task to endeavour to so arrange his work in order that he may be free to hold that brief when the case comes on for hearing. This often requires consummate skill and judgment on your part and sometimes it is impossible to accomplish and you have to return that brief to the solicitor. The moment it becomes apparent that there is a real danger that you may have to return a brief, you have a duty to tell the instructing solicitor of the true position so that he may decide whether to instruct some other counsel at the moment. or whether to wait a while to see whether your difficulties resolve themselves. If the case is an easy one for counsel to prepare, the solicitor can leave his decision much longer than if it is a heavy case which may take days or weeks to prepare. If a brief has to be returned, the solicitor may ask you whether you have another Counsel who will be free to take the case. Be ready to give him every assistance but do not thrust someone at him and never recommend one of your other counsel unless you are confident that his ability is such that he can conduct that particular case competently. Here again, some cases are so simple that the most inexperienced of counsel cannot go wrong, but it is far better to recommend counsel from another set of chambers than risk your goodwill by a careless recommendation. Never forget the duty you owe to the lay client whose liberty may be at stake or who may fail to obtain justice because you have failed to follow the strict path of duty. Some may think that I am setting the standard required of us too high in all of these things I have mentioned. When you are dealing with the general public in its pursuit of justice or in the safeguarding of the liberty of the subject, it is impossible to set the standard too high. You will find after many years of experience that solicitors often approach you to make suggestions of Counsel in cases because the barrister's clerk knows very often much better than anyone else not only the worth and ability of most of the barristers practising on his Circuit or in his particular area of work. but also has the added advantage of being able to find out through his immediate contact with other Counsel's clerks, the availability or otherwise of those barristers. Solicitors rely greatly upon us for this sort of service, and it is part of our independent role in which we maintain such pride.

'He was at once his clerk.' That means that every person who wanted Mr. Salt K.C.'s assistance had to go to a solicitor who would then go to John Lamb, the clerk, and the latter would then agree what fee Mr. Salt, K.C., was to be paid and arrange for him to appear in court or settle a will or write an opinion, or whatever the business was. He would then collect and bank the fee.

'His good servant.' Still today many barristers regard their clerk as their servant and if you get called on to do some menial task, do it with a good heart as it is part of the tradition.

'His dresser.' You see that every day in every robing room and you take care to see he has a good supply of clean collars and bands. Dressing your men who are Queen's Counsel for the Lord Chancellor's breakfast and for court levees requires expert knowledge.

'His friend.' Well, the relationship between a barrister and his clerk often is most remarkable. Thrown together so constantly as they are, a bond grows up between them that is difficult to describe – it has to be experienced.

'His flapper.' That has beaten most people. It must refer to the fact that in those days wigs were powdered and after the powdering the excess had to be flapped away. It is just possible you may escape that particular task.

'His guide.' He told him where to go and how to get there.

'His stop watch.' He told him when to go.

'His auditor.' He supervised his finances.

'His treasurer.' You, like John Lamb, will always have £20 ready in your hand for when your Principal suddenly says: 'Good heavens, I've got no money.'

'He did nothing without consulting him.' This is true today, whether the decision is something comparatively trivial or something momentous: 'Ought I to give up this type of work? Am I getting too fat? Ought I to apply to the Lord Chancellor to be made a Queen's Counsel?' The right answer to two at least of these questions depends on whether you have acquired the skill which you ought to have done after this series of lectures.

'Or failed in anything without expecting and fearing his admonishing.' Well, I advise you to go easy on this. Don't start the admonishing tomorrow morning or else your attendance at these lectures may become slightly unnecessary! Wait about twenty years.

Finally 'He resigned his title almost to respect as a master, if his clerk could ever have forgotten for a moment that he was his servant.' This is most important. It is true of many barristers today. My advice is to treasure his friendship by never forgetting your place. Nobody knows where the line is, but you will immediately know if either you or he steps over it.

Another thing you should always have in the forefront of your mind is that much you are told in chambers you are told in strict confidence. Take a pride in never divulging a confidence to anyone in the world. Let your Principal know by experience that he can speak to you without the fear of the slightest possibility of his confidence being betrayed.

One of the most interesting happenings **to** counsel's clerk is when he receives into his chambers a young man just called to the Bar who is coming in for six or twelve months as a pupil to one of the members of the chambers. He pays his master a fee, he pays the clerk a fee. He is constantly with his master either in conferences or in court. The clerk sees that he does not miss any opportunity of any new experience and imparts scraps of knowledge from his store which he has garnered over the years. If the pupil has the ability and good sense to make himself indispensable, as a result he may be given a seat, that is, made a member of the chambers. The clerk then has the pleasure of seeing the young man's practice grow.

He can use the young man to help other members of the chambers. This introduces him to solicitors who in turn make use of the young man and so his career is launched. Careful handling by the clerk at this time, such as not allowing him to run before he can walk, can be invaluable. The fortunes of the clerk and the young man are linked by the fee system; it is in both their interests that the career should succeed and many a successful counsel has enjoyed a close friendship with his clerk year in year out for the whole of his career. If, after he has been practising for ten years, his practice has grown enough, he and his clerk may decide that he ought to write a letter to the Lord High Chancellor asking that he be recommended to the Queen to be appointed Queen's Counsel. It is a tremendous decision to have to take. If it is granted it means giving up all of his junior practice and in future never appearing in court unless the case is important enough, or the client rich enough, to also brief a junior counsel with him. Neither is he allowed to settle pleadings without the assistance of a junior. Incidentally he gives up his junior counsel's gown and wears a silk one, hence the term 'he has taken silk.' The clerk's skill is required as much as ever to build up his new practice as a Queen's Counsel and if they succeed the day may come when counsel's success is crowned by elevation to the High Court Bench. Even then on many occasions the combination has not been broken and the clerk has followed his man on to the Bench as clerk to the judge.

The English legal system and the integrity of its personnel are the envy of the world. A combination such as I have just described makes no small contribution to the success of that system. Some half-informed individuals have said the clerk has too much power. The power is essential to the system and is good. It would be the misuse of the power which would be bad. Remember that members of counsel's chambers are not children and if their clerk misused his power be sure that retribution would descend upon him from a very great height.

I have mentioned how difficult can be the task of arranging that your Principal is available to hold a brief which you have accepted. It may involve obtaining the co-operation and consent of your fellow clerks and of the judge's clerk or whoever is in charge of the List. In these negotiations it is essential that you should be entirely frank and place your cards clearly on the table. If you tell half-truths or try to be slick you may possibly get away with it once, but judges 'clerks' are not fools. If they know they can trust you they can be and will be of the greatest assistance to you. Mislead them and you can become a marked man. Incidentally, often they can help you more if you take the trouble to give them accurate information as to the probable length of your cases instead of wild guesses, or if you be sure to let them know of any sudden development which may affect their lists.

I have been telling you how you should conduct yourself once you become a senior clerk. The other lectures will help you to learn how to become a good junior clerk so that ultimately you will be given your chance to become a senior clerk. Can you become a member of the Bar? In Charles Dickens 'Our Mutual Friend.' Mr. Boffin put a similar question to young Blight, a dismal looking youngster who was clerk in the chambers overlooking the graveyard in the Temple. He said to him: 'Given the ordinary rate of progress, how soon do you think it will be before you become a judge?' Young Blight thought about it and said that he had not actually applied his mind to the question. 'Well, it's open for you to go in for it, isn't it?' 'Yes,' said young Blight, 'on the principle that Britons never, never, never, he supposed it was open to him to go in for it. What he wasn't sure about was if he would come out of it.' 'It is open for you to go in for it, but the number who have, and have come out of it successfully, can be counted on your fingers.'

You will pick up a great deal of law during your career. It is what Sir John Simon used to describe as 'clerk's law'. Lord Goddard once told me that Tom Barton. clerk to Mr. Justice Henstridge, was one of the finest criminal lawyers in the country, and I know a number of existing clerks, particularly some of the Chancery Clerks, whose knowledge of the law is profound.

What you are really doing is endeavouring to become a senior clerk to counsel. Is it worth succeeding? I became a senior clerk when I was just 19 and I am still a senior clerk to counsel. My status has continued to increase all the time, except for the occasional setbacks which are our known hazards, namely the loss of a principal either by death or by promotion. It is an important position to hold. It is essential to the continuation of the English Bar in the form in which it has always existed.

I hope you succeed in your ambitions and that you will look back on this series of lectures in due time and say: 'Those builders built better than they knew,' which was what Lord Goddard said once about the founders of the Barristers' Clerks' Association.

Queen's Counsel

A question often asked is the difference between a barrister and a Q.C. The Bar Council says: "A limited number of senior barristers are made Queen's Counsel as a mark of outstanding ability. They are normally instructed in very serious or complex cases. Most senior judges once practised as Q.C.s." If the queen changes to a king, the title changes to Kings Counsel or K.C.

In Ireland, the title of Q.C. is not used. The title is S.C. or Senior Counsel.

The Law Society

The Law Society is an independent professional body for solicitors in England and Wales. A bit like a union for solicitors. They provide the 'voice' for solicitors, strive for better standards, safeguard the rule of law and work to make sure no-one is above the law. They also protect everyone's right to have access to justice.

The Law Society promote England and Wales as the jurisdiction of choice and promote the vital role legal services play in our economy. They also work internationally to open up markets for their members, defend human rights at home and abroad, support members with career opportunities, provide networking events and development training.

The Institute of Barristers' Clerks

Website: www.ibc.org.uk

In England and Wales, most Barristers are self-employed individuals who work under umbrella structures that constitute Chambers. The people who are employed by Barristers' Chambers to be responsible for running their practices and diaries are called Barristers' Clerks.

A modern chambers will also often employ other support staff such as dedicated fees clerks, IT specialists, receptionists and marketing assistants. As a result, modern chambers are fully serviced operations.

A large number of clerks are members of the Institute of Barristers' Clerks (IBC) – the professional body for clerks. It is estimated that there are currently 1,200 members of the IBC. Traditionally referred to as 'the Law's middle men', clerks possess a unique skill set and fulfil a role in which they are considered to be experts in their own right. Clerking is seen as a career in itself rather than a stepping stone to becoming a Barrister.

The legal landscape has changed much in recent years and clerks, practice managers or legal executives, as some are now called, have changed with it. Until fairly recently, little was known about the role of the clerk and of the little that did exist, much was inaccurate. It is hoped that this short introduction will explain how to become a clerk and the important roles they fulfil in today's modern legal landscape.

The Institute of Barristers' Clerks now offers a BTEC qualification designed specifically for chambers clerks. Developed by Central Law Training in consultation with the IBC and approved by Pearson.

The IBC regularly advertises jobs that are available on their website at: https://www.ibc.org.uk/jobs/

The Bar Council of England and Wales

The Bar Council represents Barristers in England and Wales.

It promotes the Barristers as specialists for advocacy and advisory services. It also promotes fair access to justice for all, ethics, equality and diversity across the profession, and the development opportunities for barristers at home and abroad.

The Bar Standards Board

The Bar Standards Board, or BSB, is our regulator. They regulate barristers' chambers in England and Wales. Scotland and Northern Ireland have different systems and rules.

They are responsible for education and training requirements for becoming a barrister, continuing training requirements to ensure that barristers' skills are maintained throughout their careers, professional conduct standards, authorising organisations that focus on advocacy, litigation and specialist legal advice, monitoring the service provided by barristers and the organisations they authorise, handling complaints against barristers and taking disciplinary or other action where appropriate.

The work that they undertake is governed by The Legal Services Act 2007 as well as a number of other statutes.

The Bar Mutual Indemnity Fund

The Bar Mutual provides professional indemnity insurance to barristers in England and Wales and the Bar Standards Board authorised or licensed entities.

Barristers are normally self-employed and all self-employed barristers are required by the Bar Standards Board to take out professional indemnity insurance with Bar Mutual.

Bar Mutual provides professional indemnity insurance cover and a claims handling service. Bar Mutual is owned and controlled by its Members.

CHAPTER THREE

How it works

The Inns of Court

In London, the four Inns of Court are the professional associations for barristers in England and Wales. They are: Gray's Inn, Lincoln's Inn, Inner Temple, and Middle Temple. Barristers have to belong to one of the Inns and they choose which one they wish to join once called.[7]

The Inns of Court have supervisory and disciplinary functions for members. The Inns provide library facilities, dining facilities and professional accommodation. Each Inn has a church or chapel attached to it and is a self-contained precinct where barristers traditionally train and practise, although the growth in the legal profession, together with a desire to practise from more modern accommodations has caused many barristers' chambers to move outside the precincts of the Inns of Court recently.

---

[7]   Called, or call to the bar is described in Wikipedia as, 'The call to the bar' is a legal term of art in most common law jurisdictions where persons must be qualified to be allowed to argue in court on behalf of another party and are then said to have been 'called to the bar' or to have received a 'call to the bar'. 'The bar' is now used as a collective noun for barristers, but literally referred to the wooden barrier in old courtrooms, which separated the often-crowded public area at the rear from the space near the judges reserved for those having business with the Court. Barristers would sit or stand immediately behind it, facing the judge, and could use it as a table for their briefs.

Like many other common law terms, the term originated in England in the Middle Ages, and the *call to the bar* refers to the summons issued to one found fit to speak at the 'bar' of the royal courts. In time, English judges allowed only legally qualified men to address them on the law and later delegated the qualification and admission of barristers to the four Inns of Court. Once an Inn calls one of its members to its bar, they are thereafter a barrister. They may not, however, practise as a barrister until they have completed (or been exempted from) an apprenticeship called pupillage. After completing pupillage, they are considered to be a practising barrister with a right of audience before all courts.

Legal history

Let us start with the four Inns of Court, home to the Barristers we serve.

These days Barristers are dotted around the UK but they are all members of one of the Inns of court. The temple, featured in *The Da Vinci Code* dates back to 1185 and was run by the Knights Templars. They were ousted in the 14th century and the property was passed by the Crown to the order of St John who had no real need for it as they already owned the vast estate of Clerkenwell (an area to the north of Fleet Street). They let it to the people who taught, learnt and practised law, who about that time had been excluded from the City of London by a writ of King Henry III. They flourished and formed themselves into societies which they called the Inns of Court and somehow acquired the exclusive right to grant a right of audience, that is the right to practice in the courts, to their members.

In 1775 lawyers and clerks lived together in chambers. Um ... In that day someone wrote: "He was at once his clerk, his good servant, dresser, his friend, flapper, his guide, stop watch, auditor and treasurer. He did nothing without consulting him or failed in anything without expecting and fearing his admonishing".

Common Law

Common law is called such because it was 'common' to all the king's courts across England and Wales. It has originated in the courts of the English kings since 1066. The English legal system spread to its many colonies, which mostly retain the common law system today. These 'common law systems' use judicial precedent, and to the style of reasoning inherited from English law.

One third of the world's population live in a common law jurisdiction: Antigua and Barbuda, Australia, Bahamas, Bangladesh, Barbados, Belize, Botswana, Burma, Cameroon, Canada (except Quebec), Cyprus, Dominica, Fiji, Ghana, Grenada, Guyana, Hong Kong, India, Ireland,

Israel, Jamaica, Kenya, Liberia, Malaysia, Malta, Marshall Islands, Micronesia, Namibia, Nauru, New Zealand, Nigeria, Pakistan, Palau, Papua New Guinea, Sierra Leone, Singapore, South Africa, Sri Lanka, Trinidad and Tobago, the United Kingdom (including Gibraltar), the United States and Zimbabwe.

A visit to the Taxing Master

Many years ago, a visit to the Taxing Master was a terrifying prospect for any inexperienced clerk. Payment in the Crown Court system worked basically like this. If you prosecute in a criminal trial, you are paid by the Crown Prosecution Service (CPS) and if you defend the Crown Court dealt with the payment to the defendant barrister.

We used to have two types of forms, red corner and green corner. Green corner forms were for what was known as standard fees, so you just claimed for what work you had undertaken and the court paid it with little or no discussion. A red corner form was intended to be for 'exceptional' cases, either due to complexity or preparation.

I recall when one of the 'red corner' forms was for a difficult case involving a lot of complex work and substantial preparation. We submitted our form to the court for consideration and the court reduced the fees considerably. Once notified of the court's view, the barrister was informed and as you can imagine the clerk gets the flack. The response was always an immediate request for the clerk to complete an appeal and send the original form, the court's decision and counsel's grounds of appeal off to the regional taxing master for a review. This was one such occasion.

Due to being inexperienced, I over-prepared, wrote out all my grounds of appeal, set out the hourly rates I had applied, details of the barrister and his specific experience, calculated the hourly rate times the preparation and in my opinion, did a fantastic job. So I thought.

I had to drive to Cardiff to meet the regional Taxing Master for the South West. Suit and tie, large file of papers, fully prepared I entered the room of the Taxing Master fearing one of the most difficult things I had done to date in my career. The Taxing Master was a lovely chap, very friendly and just doing his job so I opened my file and began to explain the detail of the case.

The Taxing Master suggested I just stop for a moment while he explained something to me. He then proceeded to explain that the barrister in question was someone he had come across in the past. He explained that before his promotion to taxing master, he was an usher in a court in the south west and he had met this barrister once before. He proceeded to tell me how rude the barrister had been to him early in his career, how arrogant and nasty he had been. He said, and I remember it so clearly to this day: "I can tell you now, your appeal will not succeed, I have been waiting for this moment for many years, so you can close your file."

I said: "Fair enough" because he was right and I had to laugh. We went to the pub, had a beer and spent a few hours talking about old times. It was a lovely afternoon in Cardiff.

When I returned to chambers the barrister in question was waiting in the clerks room for the decision. I explained that I had been fully prepared, presented all the arguments, set out everything but unfortunately, the Taxing Master was not having any of it and my appeal was dismissed. The barrister thanked me for trying and we went off for a beer.

Early days of public or direct access[8] to barristers

A colleague of mine once told me he worked at a chambers which had just started doing public access work. Two businessmen came in for a conference with one of the commercial barristers. He always thought the

---

[8]   The Public Access Scheme (a.k.a. 'Direct Access') allows members of the public in England and Wales to instruct a barrister directly. In the past, it was necessary for clients to use a solicitor or other third party in order to instruct a barrister. It was first established in 2004. The scheme heralded the first time for more than a century that barristers could be instructed directly by the public without the involvement of a solicitor, and there was a level of uncertainty as to whether clients would understand the limitations of barristers' work.

direct relationship could be a difficult one and as he walked past the conference room no more than five minutes after they arrived, he heard the barrister irate and shouting at the top of his voice ... 'If you want that, why don't you just get a f ... ing solicitor!'

Suffice to say he thinks it was that particular barrister's only toe in the water with public access work!

Thankfully since 2004, the barristers have undertaken further training and now deal with members of the public as a growing part of their work.

Direct access to barristers by members of the public is now 25% of the Bar's income. Today, over half of the 12,000 barristers in England and Wales have undertaken further training and deal directly with the public, in addition to solicitors and other lawyers.

How can a barrister defend someone they know is guilty?

Often when I explain what I do for a job I am asked: "How can a barrister defend someone they know is guilty?" Well, the answer is quite simple, they cannot. If a client tells you they are guilty, you cannot represent them at a trial of not guilty.

The key point here is that they don't tell you they are guilty, they tell you they are innocent and it is the barrister's job to represent them and present the case as best as they can.

One of our senior criminal barristers once said to me: "If you were walking along with your wife and someone ran past, stabbed her and ran off into the darkness, you try to pull the knife from her so your hands are on the knife, you are covered in blood and someone turns the corner

---

Over the course of numerous consultations conducted by the Bar Standards Board, the rules for public access practice were gradually relaxed to serve the public interest, particularly in the light of pending cuts to Legal Aid funding The current Public Access rules, which enable the widest scope of direct public access to barristers to date, are covered in C119-C131 of the Code of Conduct contained in the Bar Standards Board Handbook which came into force on 15 April 2015.

and sees you standing over her, hand on knife, covered in blood would you want your barrister to believe you? Add to that scenario, you had an argument in a very public place earlier so everyone knows you were upset with her. If that were you, however bad it looks, you would be delighted that your barrister accepts what you say, looks at it objectively and presents your defence to the judge." It does happen.

CHAPTER FOUR

Life in chambers

What are chambers?

Barristers work together in 'Chambers'. The model has existed for a very long time as it is a sharing of expenses. A barrister working on his or her own could not afford the offices, marketing, IT and staff so they gather together to form a chambers and share the common expenses.

Barristers are self-employed (sole practitioners) so they work together from chambers employing the clerks.

Most chambers are held together with a 'constitution' rather than a partnership agreement as they have historically not been allowed to form partnerships. Nowadays, more modern business structures are permitted so various forms of alternative business structures are emerging and being permitted.

Chambers constitution

Every barristers chambers should have a written constitution which sets out a description of its management structure. A constitution is normally only varied with the approval of a chambers meeting. Less significant matters are recorded in the chambers manual or other chambers' documentation. The written constitution and description of management structure would normally include things like the decision-making structure, and include the duties and authority of the Head of Chambers and the Management Committee.

Other details will include things like the frequency, purpose of and arrangements for attendance at periodic chambers meetings, financial structure and responsibilities, including the arrangements and policy for the payment of chambers rent,[9] also arrangements for the remuneration of clerks and other members of chambers staff, arrangements and policy for payment of other expenses, authority to enter into commitments on behalf of chambers, or individual tenants,[10] practice management for the bar and arrangements for the entry of new tenants to and the departure of tenants from chambers, including periods of notice and liabilities of incoming and outgoing tenants. It also includes details of the ownership of and liability for assets and property used by chambers, policy and arrangements for the fair and just resolution of disputes within chambers including, where appropriate, reference to the Bar Council's arbitration scheme and the obligation which Members of Chambers have to comply with the terms of all contracts, policies, codes or quality standards agreed or entered into by Chambers, teams or groups within Chambers.

As you can see, it is quite an important document and in my experience one that causes endless meetings and discussion, arguments and fall outs in a traditional chambers.

---

[9] Rent is the term used in chambers for the fees barristers pay towards the running costs of chambers. There are various models for paying rent. Some chambers have a straight percentage, like our chambers, Clerksroom. Our members pay 15% of income towards our costs. Other chambers will have fixed fees or a mix of percentage and fixed fees. Each chambers decides what level of chambers rent to set, trying to balance the budget between the estimated costs for running chambers and the likely income. Most chambers will appoint one barrister as a treasurer who reports on the budget and rent payments to chambers meeting. If there is a budget excess, it is normally returned to the barristers at year end.

[10] Tenant – barristers who work from a chambers are called 'Tenants' of the chambers. A door tenant (or associate member) is a barrister who has been granted permission to join an additional set of chambers and also work with them from premises. A 'Squatter' is a fully qualified barrister who has finished his/her training but has not been invited to join the chambers. They are not tenants, so they are using the facilities and called squatters until they find a chambers to practise from and become a full tenant.

One chambers meeting[11]

Important Chambers Business ... Agenda, Item 1 ... Square teabags, not round   Need I say more!

From Punch, July–December 1845

"We have now nothing left but the barrister's clerk, who derives life consequence or the reverse from the standing at the bar or the utter brieflessness of his employer. A barrister's clerk should never expose the professional secrets of his master; but if a client should come with even a simple motion of course, the clerk should search a large book containing an imaginary list to see whether We – for the Barrister's Clerk usually says we – are retained for the other side. If you have nothing to do at chambers, you may endorse some dummies with tremendous ideal fees in very large figures, and write in a very legible hand, 'WITH YOU, MR. ATTORNEY-GENERAL,' or 'CONSULTATION AT THE SOLICITOR-GENERAL'S CHAMBERS AT SIX,' and these should be left lying in such a position that everyone who comes into the chambers cannot avoid seeing them. If your master's practice is so notoriously nominal that this 'dodge' could not by any possibility succeed, you, who are his clerk, will probably be a boy, and you will require juvenile recreation. For this purpose there is the whole of the Temple, where pitch-and-toss may be played at all reasonable hours with any other juvenile clerk who may be disposed for the pastime alluded to. One of the greatest accomplishments of a barrister's clerk consists in knowing how to shirk attendance at chambers, and what notices placed on the door are the best adapted to lull suspicion. 'Return in an hour' is a standard rule in all cases of vagueness, for the chance of your coming hack is so void for remoteness, that few would come to test the validity of the document at the time when you have made yourself returnable. 'Gone to Westminster' looks extremely well upon the door, and may apply to your master as well as to

---

[11] Chambers are organised by committees, chambers have a lot of meetings. Everything is discussed and agreed by committee.

47

TALES OF A BARRISTERS' CLERK

yourself. So that when you know he is either fishing or shooting in the country, and is sure not to come back and find you out, you may put up the notice alluded to with credit to all parties."

Gas lamps in Temple

Would you like to see the last remaining working gas lamps in London? British Gas light them every night with: 'Ye Olde Lamplighters', who carry out this traditional function every day in London. Find our more at www.BritishGas.co.uk/the-source/lamplighters. The map does not include Temple as it is private land but the original gas lamps still exist and they are lit by the British Gas lamplighters each day.

When your son says will you ask the Prime Minister's wife for an autograph ...

I told my seven-year-old son (Toby) at bedtime one evening that I was going to meet the Prime Minister's wife the next day at a function in London. I would be there, she would be there, and I knew her clerk really well (the Prime Minister's wife is a Q.C.) so I thought we would probably have a chat.

He immediately replied by saying that was cool and asked if I could take his autograph book with me and get her to sign it. Now, how do you break it to a seven-year-old that it is not quite what you do at a chambers party? But I said I would try. The biggest problem I had was the autograph book in question was a David Beckham autograph book with nothing in it to date. It had been a Christmas gift and my son was pretty keen to get something in it.

The next day at the chambers party I summoned up the courage to ask for the signature in the David Beckham autograph book and it was duly done quite happily. Just as she was about to hand it back to me she stopped, took it back and said, "Why not leave it with me, I'm seeing my husband tonight on the way to Chequers and I'll tell him to sign it too. Come to think of it, most of the cabinet will be there this weekend so I'll get them all to sign it, send messages to Toby and then post it back to you Monday."

It arrived back on the Wednesday with a lovely note for my son who was over the moon. Some people really are lovely.

Who can we get to open our new building?

When we started Clerksroom (with two barristers and me) we designed a purpose-built chambers building for our new venture. We started the chambers in 2001 and moved into our new building in 2003. We wanted to have a grand opening party, so we invited the then Prime

Minister's wife and some law lords to declare the building open.

One of our barristers, Dr Michael Powers Q.C. is also a helicopter pilot so he offered to fly his jet helicopter up to Battersea Heliport to collect the Prime Minister's wife, fly her to Somerset and return her after the event in time for an evening function.

Everything was organised which included getting Civil Aviation approval to fly over the M5, land in our car park at Blackbrook Park Avenue in Taunton, bring down the Downing Street protection officers from Scotland Yard who have to travel everywhere too, obtain special permission from the Avon and Somerset Police who would provide special protection (armed) officers in Taunton to cover the 50-yards between the helicopter landing spot and the entrance to our building. Everyone had to be security vetted, the building had to be 'swept' twice, the helicopter needed another paid pilot as it is a jet and cannot be flown by just one pilot I was told, then we had to pay for the fuel (ouch) and we needed clearance to land at Exeter to park and re-fuel. All pretty straightforward and just another day in the office for a clerk.

The helicopter duly landed, the builders working opposite were a bit surprised by who stepped out, the kids at the Kiddi Caru nursery next to our building were all out front to watch the helicopter land and were amazed by the passenger, who then went over, shook hands with all the builders and kids before declaring our office open.

I thought I had planned everything but when I asked what she would like to drink she replied, "Lapsang Souchong please". I have to admit to not

6   SOMERSET COUNTY GAZETTE, MARCH 5, 2004   www.thisisthewestcountry.co.uk/somerset

There's no dispute: Cherie loves Taunton

THE UK's first lady. Cherie Booth QC flew in by helicopter to help celebrate the opening of a new facility in Taunton on Monday.

The Prime Minister's wife, who uses her maiden name in her professional life as a barrister, was among the guests at the official opening of the £1.2million ADR Chambers in Blackbrook.

Retired law lord Lord Browne-Wilkinson officially opened the ADR Chambers UK and Europe Case Management and Mediation Centre on Monday as a host of VIPs from the legal world and local dignitaries attended.

The global company has scores of famous legal names on its books and is promoting mediation as a better way of settling disputes than using the courts.

A mediator such as Cherie Booth is called in when both sides of a dispute — anything from warring neighbours to big businesses — agree to talk.

The idea is that parties sit down in a less formal or costly environment than the courts and come to a mutual agreement that can be far more flexible than a court ruling.

Mediation is backed by the Government because it takes the pressure off the court system.

In an interview with the County Gazette she described Taunton as "a most beautiful part of the country" and spoke briefly about life at Number 10.

She said: "Mediation is all about allowing people to take ownership of their disputes. It's not just the legal rights and wrongs — it's about a continuing relationship.

"It's been successful so far — I held a mediation session this morning and we reached an amicable agreement.

"Basing this facility in Taunton is a real example of technology transforming the legal practice.

"I've been to Taunton before on various visits - it really is a most beautiful part of the world."

On how she juggles life as the Prime Minister's wife, a mother of four, and an eminent barrister, she said: "Law practice is what keeps me sane."

And on life in Downing Street she said: "It's as great as it has always been."

ADR Chambers is also making its state-of-the-art facilities available to certain charities in the local area.

■ **PICTURE:** From left, Taunton Deane's Mayor Andrew Govier, Cherie Booth, barrister and mediator Jonathan Dingle, Mayoress Jackie Govier and Lord Browne-Wilkinson.

having thought about that or asking in advance what she drank. Seeing the look on my face, she kindly produced a tea bag from her handbag and handed it over saying, "I always bring my own". Thank goodness for that. Afterwards we bought a box of exotic teas from Twinings and now have a stock should any other like-minded people pop in.

Pupillage

Pupillages are split into two different phases. The 'first six' (months) involves observing the pupil's supervisor at court, in conference, and assisting with related paperwork. In many chambers, this is the more relaxed part of the pupillage, as the pupil has little responsibility.

In the second six months of pupillage, each pupil is responsible for a personal caseload. This will range from a first appearance in the County Court or Magistrates' Court, hearings in the High Court, or to full trials. Some 'second-six' pupils may gain experience of jury trials, but this is extremely rare. Generally speaking most second six pupils handle minor proceedings such as case management conferences, plea and directions hearings, infant settlements or small claims cases, such as possession hearings, debt recovery proceedings or road traffic claims.

The amount of work that a pupil gains in the second six depends on the chambers. Second six pupils in criminal sets are typically in court several times a week, while pupils in civil sets may have only two or three cases in a week. Second six pupils in commercial sets can go their entire pupillage without ever appearing in court.

In most leading criminal and civil sets, pupils receive a frequent supply of work. However, as clerks do not prioritize pupils it may take some time before they are paid for their work. In some cases, pupils will never be paid for the work carried out in court. This has led to a situation where pupils struggle to make ends meet, especially in criminal sets.

To attain membership of one of the Inns of Court and to be called to the Bar pupils need to eat dinners. The final qualification to becoming a barrister is to attend a dozen formal dinners held at the four Inns of

Court in London. The medieval ritual has its roots in the days when the four Inns (Inner Temple, Middle Temple, Lincoln's and Gray's) were responsible for vocational legal education. All would lodge in them, attend lectures, take part in mock courts and dine together in the Inns' main halls. Today barristers' professional training is conducted by private law schools around the country, but the dinners live on.

Truro court users committee meeting

Most courts in England and Wales have a court users committee which is made up of anyone who uses the court on a regular basis. It will include the Crown Prosecution Service,[12] barristers, clerks, solicitors and members of organisations like the Citizens Advice Bureau. It is an opportunity to speak to judges, courts staff and share ideas.

I was a member of most court users committees in the South West while working as a senior clerk in Taunton. One such meeting was in Truro.

The judge in charge of the court is called the presiding judge and he had invited all court users to attend a special meeting to ask for feedback and what people thought of the court. What the judge did not realise was that his official letter to everyone on the court database had gone out to a prisoner in Dartmoor who did not have a solicitor, so he was the client himself (people who don't use lawyers are called Litigants in Person or LIPs as lawyers call them). So a letter from the presiding judge of Truro Crown Court had been sent to the LIP in Dartmoor Prison inviting him to attend the special meeting of the Court Users Committee and tell the judge what he thought of the judge and court.

HMP Dartmoor had no choice but to arrange transport and officers to take him to court for 5pm when the meeting was due to take place.

---

12 The Crown Prosecution Service or CPS, is the public agency responsible for criminal prosecutions in England and Wales. The head is the Director of Public Prosecutions (DPP). The role of the CPS is to provide advice to the police and investigative agencies during criminal investigations, they decide if a suspect should face charges following an investigation, and they conduct prosecutions both in the magistrates' courts and the Crown Court.

The prisoner was escorted into the court room being used to hold the meeting and the meeting began. When asked who would like to be first to give feedback the prisoner put his hand up, and was invited to speak. The prisoner told the judge clearly, in no uncertain terms, what he thought of him and his court before being led away back to the waiting prison van for him to be returned to Dartmoor. The judge seemed a bit confused as to how this had come about.

Guernsey is nice!

Atkin Chambers in London used to work shifts for the clerks, early and late so the clerks room was staffed 8am to 7pm. It was a Friday night in the summer and one of the barristers came down to the clerks room and announced that his papers for his huge arbitration were packed up and ready to be taken to Guernsey for a 9am start Monday morning.

We all knew he had the big case on Monday but he had not mentioned to anyone that the papers needed to be taken there. All can be solved by a call to our courier company who would collect, package and send by DHL. I think it was about 3pm and the couriers informed us that they could not send packages by air unaccompanied, someone would need to go with them and that was going to cost a small fortune.

After much head scratching and discussion of ideas, I offered to take them over to Guernsey myself. I called Claire who worked in East Croydon, she managed to get away from her job early and met me on the train.

The papers were in six large bankers boxes so I took them in a taxi to Victoria Station, loaded them onto the train to Redhill where we were living, unloaded them in Redhill, Claire waited at the station and I fetched the car. We drove to Poole in Dorset, jumped on the Condor overnight ferry and arrived at a very early time Saturday morning. Each of the heavy boxes had to be carried from the ferry to a distance I could see, and then I marched them up into town one by one.

It was one of those very hot days in the summer and was already hot at 7am in the Channel Islands. Once the papers were delivered to the hotel, we spent the day on the beach, overnight in a hotel and caught the ferry home Sunday ready for work on Monday. My total bill for the petrol, ferry, hotel, meals etc worked out much cheaper than the courier would have cost and we had an adventure with a night on Guernsey.

I'm going to blow up your chambers

When someone tells you they are going to blow up your chambers you do tend to worry a bit and hope that they are not really serious, just perhaps having a bad day.

During my days at South Western Chambers one day a client told us he would blow up chambers and we did decide to take it seriously. What made the threat more meaningful was that when he had turned up in chambers for a conference with his defence barrister he had opened his briefcase to get out his papers and it was full of hand grenades. Now, this is a true story, it happened to me; I was there.

The background was that Mr. Edwards had been charged with the supply of arms and he attended chambers for a conference so clearly he was on bail. I took some coffees into the meeting and the barrister had a white face. As the client had opened his briefcase the barrister could not fail to notice it was full of hand grenades and asked him to close the case and he would pretend he had never seen them. The client remarked that they were very easy to buy, there is an antiques shop in Frome where you can buy them. Moving swiftly on, the barrister completed the conference and the trial was set for a few weeks' time.

The trial date came and lasted for about a week. The defendant was duly convicted and sent down. The defendant did not take kindly to the sentence and immediately leapt out of the dock at Taunton Crown Court and duly punched the barrister in the face. He was wrestled to the floor by two court security guards and was quickly dispatched to the cells where you can move a prisoner from the court cell block under the road and over to the police station. I think that has now been closed but you could at that time.

As he was leaving the court he shouted back to the barrister: "When I get out of prison, I will blow up your chambers," in full view of the judge, the security and the police officers who had just secured a conviction. He said it without doubt! The police asked the barrister if he wished to press charges, the barrister declined and therefore no paperwork was required, just a beer, or two, or three. That was the end of the matter, or so we thought.

Several months later, I drove into chambers very early (for me) to find a car in the car park already which was familiar and I knew I had seen it before. As it was not one of my barristers' cars who could it be? I racked my brains for half an hour and as nobody was in chambers that morning it was just bugging me that it was strange and certainly not normal. THEN I REMEMBERED!

The last time I had seen that car Mr. Edwards was in chambers for a conference with his Barrister – the hand grenade man and the same one who said he would blow up chambers when he was out of prison. To say I panicked is a mild understatement, I was totally terrified. Nothing like this has ever happened to me before, my job is not normally life or death. Yes, a barrister can be late for court and we have to apologise to a client but nobody dies. I was truly scared. I called the police, they reacted immediately. I will never forget it – police sealed off the road each side of chambers, bomb squad in full kit, helicopter and all kicking off as the barristers arrived for the day. I advised everyone they could not go into chambers and the phones were left to ring for the first time in my career. This was serious.

I was asked by the police where was the barrister in question and I told them he was at Taunton Crown Court. They asked me to go to the court to warn him. Because the police wanted it to be discreet I called ahead to the door security to alert them to the panic and explained the helicopter overhead. As I arrived at court, my worst nightmare was happening, Mr. Edwards was sitting calmly in the waiting area just inside the court building. A plain clothes CID officer and I asked the security staff who he was (even though I knew only too well he was Mr. Edwards) and said that my Barrister (Mr Edwards' previous counsel) was in the robing room. Mobile phone call to barrister to say stay in the robing room, do not leave, we have a situation here and you are in grave danger. Seemed right at the time. The security office checked the records and I was right, Mr. Edwards had checked in under a false name. Ten minutes later, while the special armed officers assembled outside, I kept out of the way, as any self-respecting coward would. The special police team went in, decked him and carried him out, over the road to the police station and he was in the cells.

Phew, we had escaped near death. Back to chambers, all was well, rather shocked but had to press on with the work that was now getting urgent.

Later my mate, Andrew, a retired police officer with Yeovil CID popped over to Taunton custody office and asks the custody officer what happened and had Mr. Edwards been charged. The custody serjeant who was a good friend of his replied: "Why do you want to know?" He informed the chief constable and said they had no record of anyone being brought in that day. Strange. Yeovil CID told me later he was wanted by a much higher authority than them and my tip off and visual confirmation had sparked a major police manhunt to which they were truly grateful as this chap had been avoiding them since his release from prison which was allowed as part of the operation.

So all was well that ends well. That evening I was in the Sanctuary Wine Bar opposite chambers relaying the day's events to some of my barristers over a pint of Grolsch and one of my juniors asked me what was the car that had caused all the chaos? I explained which one it was and he just looked at me and said: "Oh, that's my hire car, my Porsche is in for service and they loaned me that car for the day".

It turned out Mr Edwards had sold the car to the garage when he went to prison and the garage had decided to use it as a courtesy car. I actually feel rather sorry for Mr. Edwards as it turned out he was at court with his girlfriend to help her with her custody case and had to use a false name as he was a wanted man.

Party night at South Western Chambers, Taunton

Our German friends

One of our barristers, Theo Pangraz, moved from Germany where he was a Rechtsanwalt, the German equivalent of barrister.

Theo was able to transfer to the Bar of England and Wales as he was a qualified European Lawyer and so the transfer is reasonably easy. Once Theo had moved from Hamburg to London, we began working together and I looked after him as normal.

One of the oddities of working in the courts of England and Wales as a European Lawyer is that you can appear in a court but you cannot wear the traditional wig and gown that barristers wear in court. On one occasion, Theo was in court and the judge put his fingers in his ears and looked at Theo and said loudly: "I cannot hear you". Theo was a bit bemused and after a while the judge was pretty cross and said that Theo was not dressed properly before him, he should be wearing his wig and gown and therefore, he could not hear him.

The court session is called a hearing and the parties are heard by the judge, so the judge was saying Theo could not appear before him improperly dressed and needed to put his wig and gown on if he wanted to be heard. Theo explained to the judge that he was a European qualified lawyer and was not permitted to wear a wig and gown at that time. The judge, clearly not knowing the rules, adjourned the case so he could call the Bar Standards Board and ask for advice. He arrived back in court, sat down and said carry on. No apology to Theo or his client for what was a bizarre situation and then at the end of the hearing, he said to Theo that next time he came back into court, he should wear traditional dress. Theo replied that he would certainly wear his lederhosen next time and they left. I am not sure the Judge found it very amusing but Theo did.

Pink Tape

Various stories abound as to why pink or red tape is used to keep lawyers' papers together in a bundle.

Historically, instructions presented to a barrister from a solicitor, known as a brief, were surrounded by a 'backsheet' and folded in a particular way, secured with a pink ribbon or tape. The backsheet is used to record the outcome of the hearing and the papers were returned to the solicitor after a hearing with the result handwritten on the backsheet. Sometimes the 'brief' will be passed to another counsel when there are multiple hearings, so the handwritten notes by each barrister informs the next of the progress of the matter.

The fee for the barristers' appearance at court – the Brief Fee – was recorded in ink on the backsheet before any hearing. This ensured that the fee agreed between the clerk and the instructing solicitor, on occasions, could be inspected by the Judge when costs were being considered, to ensure that a fee had been agreed in advance – in accordance with the rules at the time – and not enhanced after the hearing when the barrister had succeeded in getting a good financial result in the event of a civil claim, for example.

Nobody knows exactly where and why the custom started, but pink ribbon has been holding legal documents together for a very long time by tradition. Back in the 16th century, it is understood that documents at the Vatican were also kept together using pink ribbon.

Another story is that Henry VIII sent his petition to the Pope for divorce from one of wives bound in pink tape which started a tradition here in England. The pink however was most likely a faded red, hence the term 'red tape', a phrase used to refer to an excessive amount of rules and processes that need to be considered, before an official action can be taken.

The English icon, Charles Dickens, is believed to be the first person to use this phrase. Pink ribbon may be the most recognisable, but other colours are often used in the legal profession and in proceedings. White tape used to be regularly used around briefs from the Crown e.g. Treasury Solicitor. Pink tape is after all, white tape dyed pink, so the Crown were just using a more economic tape. Green ribbon has been used for many years to sew up court documents, and black ribbon is still sometimes used for probate papers.

Freemasonry and barristers' clerks

Many male barristers' clerks and administrators are members of Free-masonry. Freemasonry is an International organisation which has been in existence for many centuries. It is not a secret society. It is a society with secrets – they relate to the ceremonies which freemasons take part in which are designed to teach morals in a progressive manner – by degrees.

Membership is open to any man of 'mature age' who wishes to be part of a society that promotes charitable works. Famous people that have been known to be Freemasons include Churchill and several Presidents of the USA. The Royal Family have always had close ties with Free-masonry, and the present Duke of Kent has been the Grand Master of the order since 1967.

Freemasonry in London alone has contributed millions of pounds to charity. In recent years, among the various charitable grants made, London Freemasons were responsible for paying for the second emergency helicopter that now operates over London, and are currently funding a special fire engine with a turntable ladder that will be able to navigate London's narrow streets and save lives (in the aftermath of the Grenfell Tower fire).

Freemasons are grouped together in 'Lodge's' and typically meet four times a year, for a meeting which usually includes a 'degree' ceremony followed by a dinner where there are plenty of speeches and toasts, raffles and laughter.

Many famous barristers' clerks have been members of the Lodge's associated with the legal profession. Templars Lodge and Equity Lodge both have current or past members and officers of the Institute of Barristers' Clerks, including many past chairmen.

One of the most significant parts of being a Freemason and a barristers' clerk, is that Freemason meetings give an opportunity for work colleagues to meet as friends and socialise away from work as well as helping the wider community.

Although written from a male perspective, female barristers' clerks can also be Freemasons, although women Freemasonry is run by a totally separate organisation.

Recent times

Things have not honestly changed much.

The profession has undergone a huge change, expecting clerks to be masters of IT, marketing, property, management, and still the traditional clerk looking after the barristers every request. The reality is that something has to give and clerks have had to adapt to meet the demands of their new modern masters, while trying to cling on to what is good about the clerking profession.

The days of long afternoons in the Temple pubs with friendly solicitors (what do they call it ... Marketing!) have long gone.

Today

Barristers' chambers are now multi-million-pound businesses. Some are still quaint and old school, they are unlikely to stay around much longer.

Who knows – they may do and if they enjoy it, enjoy the old way of life, and make it pay – that is great.

Most modern barristers' chambers now employ staff who manage IT, marketing, credit control and hospitality but they leave the clerking to the team who have been selected based on experience and communications skills. The exact skill of a clerk is very difficult to pinpoint. A good barristers' clerk has to be able to communicate effectively, provide a high level of client care to some of the most demanding clients ever (who are often in very pressurised environments and have tight deadlines to meet). They need to be fair, understand the regulations that govern the legal profession, know a little about the wide variety of areas of law that could be discussed and do this whilst taking telephone calls, reviewing faxes, answering emails and speaking to clients who call in to say hello and want to chat. Then there are the Barristers – in our case 125 of them. They like to chat! They also like to let you know how they got on in court, what happened to them on the way to court, how eventful their journey home was, what pressure they are under and, of course, an in-depth explanation of the interesting points of law they went into at court.

Before they go to court, we need to firstly undertake some marketing, manage the client relationship with the barrister and take account of the relationships others in chambers have with the firm they work for. Then we need to advise the solicitors who call us on the most suitable barrister for the work, note it all in the electronic diary and set up a case file with all the notes of conversations, court details, client letters and so on. We need to agree some fees for the barrister so we need to be masters of estimation without any papers, ideas of what is involved or the complexity of the case. But we tend to get it right more often than not – I'm not exactly sure how ...

Marketing complete, communications fine, diary sorted – the papers arrive for the case. We need to complete the computerised file, scan in any relevant papers, read through them to make sure there is no further key information contained inside the papers, then when we are sure – take a deep breath and pass them to the barrister to work on. While that's happening, the dates are checked with the court and the barristers' diary is checked to make sure they know where and when to attend court, which judge and how they should dress – open court or in chambers (wigs and gowns or suits). If we go to court with Counsel, we carry the bag to the robing room, take the papers for the case to the right court, hand in lists of authorities and pour the barrister (and his leader or junior) a glass of water. Sometimes it does get exciting because things happen – like the barrister forgot his shoes and is left in trainers just about to appear in a big case – you think I've just made that up! Well, unfortunately not. Getting a shoe shop to open early and deliver a pair of size 11 formal shoes to a court puts a good clerk to the test.

Now – this is where it can all go pear shaped!

If all goes to plan, the barrister completes the work on time as agreed, spends a proportionate amount of time on the papers and we are about right with the fee. So we get them back to sort out again, the papers are tidied up, sorted back to the original state they came in and the work is added to the computer system, an invoice produced, the work stored on the case file and the papers go back in the post or the DX to the solicitor with the invoice. Credit control then send a few rude letters and 12-18 months down the line after various excuses and attempts to wriggle out of paying the agreed fee, the cheque arrives. A few excuses including I'm unable to get to the file at the moment as it is exactly the right size to prop up my desk so it is difficult to get to.

Now, once the cheque has been banked and cleared – and only at that point, you obtain client feedback. If the feedback is OK, you can speak to the solicitor again and if all goes to plan, they send some more work in due course. It all starts again.

The future

Ever since I started making tea and pushing a trolley load of books from the Temple to the High Court, one barrister or another has told me the end of the profession is nigh. But it has not happened. I am an optimist so I prefer to think that the profession may just get a wonderful opportunity one day to demonstrate what a great profession it is.

It is in fact a streamlined profession, very professional with a huge amount of pro-bono work being undertaken for the greater good. But that's not sexy and newspapers and politicians like to be seen to shake things up a bit. What is needed is a compromise, in my opinion, a bit of a shake-up but not too much as we risk spoiling a great profession.

I suspect lawyers will merge at some time and some barristers will be excited by the prospects of working for the larger firms of solicitors. I suspect that the number of barristers' chambers in the UK will greatly reduce and the average size of chambers will increase. The number of clerks is likely to remain about the same and increase gradually as the number of barristers gradually increases.

London will always be the capital of the legal profession but the reliance on London will diminish – but it will always be the heart of the law – no matter what is thrown at the profession. I should of course say that Taunton will be the heart of the legal profession but – er …

A few stories from David Goddard

Peter Curry Q.C. – Bahamas/Cayman/London

When I became Senior Clerk at 4 Stone Buildings Peter Curry was the Head of Chambers and in his sixties. He had had a distinguished career as a company law specialist and probably the only barrister to get silk twice.

Typical of life at the Bar things do not fit into neat boxes. If a barrister has only two cases in one year you can bet they will be on the same day. Anyway, Peter was instructed to do a three-day case in the Bahamas starting on a Monday. On the Thursday he was then booked to do a hearing in the Cayman Islands which was due to last two days. This was all to fit in with an arbitration which was fixed for the following Monday to be heard in London at Lloyd's. Peter and I discussed at length whether it would be possible to deal with such a tight schedule.

We were fortunate as the case in the Bahamas finished in two days and Peter was able to take a scheduled flight to the Cayman Islands. But we were not so fortunate when the Cayman case overran. Gratefully we were assisted by the court who sat on the Saturday to finish.

However, this created a difficulty with him getting a flight back to London. Apparently he would only be able to get a flight on Sunday to arrive at Heathrow at 8.30am on Monday.

On the Monday morning I telephoned Heathrow airport (no Internet then) to check whether the plane was due on time. It was. However, at 8.45am I telephoned the airport again just to make sure it had landed. It hadn't. Managed to get the hearing put back. Peter eventually arrived at the Arbitration at 11.15am having read further papers for the case in the car on route.

There were moments when I thought it would not work out and it is something I did not relish at the time. My nerves were put to the test.

I had the greatest admiration for Peter taking this on. He not only had to go between each destination but also prepare and conduct each hearing under extreme pressure. He never moaned, panicked or complained about the situation. After we had taken the decision to do it he simply got on with it. I would go as far to say he actually thrived on it. Let us not also forget this was at a time when most of Peter's solicitor contemporaries were in retirement. This summed him up as a barrister – cool, unflappable, full of energy and with tremendous stamina.

I do not believe there is anyone else at the bar, young or old, who might have undertaken such a task. In retrospect I do not think I would even recommend it to anyone or want to go through it again.

Peter is well known to a lot of clerks, particularly those in Lincoln's Inn. I also know that he has given help and guidance to other clerks. One clerk in particular tells the story when a large case with numerous silks in it was adjourned to discuss settlement he went round and asked each Silk what sandwiches they wanted. When he came to Peter, he said: "I'll have a pint of beer please," and that is how he remembers him.

Robert Maxwell

One of the first things I learnt as a clerk is the lay client does not speak to the barrister direct, only through a solicitor. Robert Maxwell telephoned chambers during my very early days as a clerk and asked to be put through to Mr. Stamler. I said he couldn't speak to him direct but he must go through his instructing solicitor. I mentioned to Sam Stamler he had called and what I had said. 20 minutes later Robert Maxwell called again and was a bit more aggressive this time. Again I told the same thing to him. He put the phone down and after a further 20 minutes he called again. Again I stood by my ground and would not put him through.

A couple of days later Robert Maxwell come into the clerks room and in a loud voice and said 'who is David Goddard!' I stood up and he said: "Hello David pleased to meet you, I am Robert Maxwell."

Leo Price Q.C.

Leo Price Q.C. and Philip Heslop Q.C. were against each other in a packed court. One of the things that needed to be sorted out was when the main hearing was to be heard so Frank Wright (Leo's clerk) and I attended court asking both our barristers to make sure this question was dealt with first so we could go back to chambers. However, Leo Price rather started to get into the case and I kept looking across to Frank. After about 15 minutes Frank finally caught Leo Price's attention whereupon he said: "My Lord I must stop the proceedings. We have two people in court far more important than any of us. They have more pressing things to deal with than to continue to listen to me etc,". It was said in a very humorous way and got the whole court laughing.

Philip Heslop Q.C. – Money to Ibiza

The things we do for barristers. Philip Heslop was on holiday in Ibiza. He had been mugged and all his money and credit cards were taken. The first person he calls is me. He was in a panic. Fortunately I knew his bank manager so got all his cards cancelled. I then managed to get some money from my bank and booked my junior clerk on a flight.

Philip Heslop Q.C. – Robes to Paris

A few years later bearing in mind I had rescued Philip Heslop in Ibiza he set me another task! Stephen Harwood had arranged a seminar/conference for French and English judges. Stephen Harwood had invited Mr Justice Millett as he was then. What Stephen Harwood had forgotten to tell him was to bring his judicial robes. "No problem," says Philip Heslop at 5pm on a Friday evening when the ceremony is on the next day with the robes are required. "Ring my clerk!" I couldn't believe the request when the call came in. I immediately called John Hale the Chancery Clerk of the Lists not actually expecting him to be there. He was. I explained my dilemma that we needed to get Mr Justice Millett's robes to Paris that night or by first thing the next morning.

It took some negotiation from John Hale and security but I met him at court and we managed to get the robes. John came back to Chambers with me and once again I wanted a junior clerk volunteer. Jason Doyle was first to offer, he actually knew Millett as he clerked him for a while when he was at Enterprise Chambers. Off to Paris Jason went, arriving around midnight to meet up with Philip Heslop. Apparently Mr. Justice Millett was amazed in the morning to find all his robes there and he could attend the ceremony in all his finery. When Philip Heslop died Lord Millett (as he then became, wrote a piece in *The Times* referring to this.

Robert Ralphs

I have only worked with two senior clerks: Reg Murrell and Robert Ralphs. I learnt a lot from both of them as they had completely different ways of clerking.

Robert Ralphs was an outstanding clerk and I doubt there will ever be anyone better and I very much enjoyed my time working with him. We had a great working relationship and he has been a good friend to me to this day. However, on one occasion when I was a lot slimmer than I am now, Robert and I had a disagreement and I would not budge in my view. He came over to me, picked me up and put me in the wastepaper basket.

CHAPTER FIVE

You have to laugh

Barristers and cars

One of our senior female barristers came into chambers in Gray's Inn one morning, she was clearly annoyed. She walked into the clerks room and announced to the clerks that she had just experienced terrible service at her local BMW dealer where she had purchased a new car. She explained there was a light on the dashboard and so she took the car back. The young mechanic in the service department came out to have a look and announced that the diagnosis was, "It's the oil light, you have to put some oil in it". I will never forget her telling the clerks, "I told the mechanic, what do I pay you for? It's under the bonnet, it's your job, I don't touch anything under there". We all felt sorry for the young mechanic who clearly had not met a barrister before or he would have handled it quite differently.

This also reminds me of another garage story, how true it is I am unsure. A barrister once went into a garage announcing to the service team, "I need some 710 please". Baffled they looked at each other and asked what it was as they had no idea. "The stuff you put in your engine stupid, 710." Still baffled, the mechanic took the barrister to the car and lifted the bonnet and said, "show me". The barrister pointed to the cap that said, "710" on it. The mechanic turned it around 180 degrees and said, "I'll go and get some OIL for you sir".

Again, not entirely sure this is true, but another clerk told me a barrister had purchased a brand-new BMW which was automatic. He drove from the garage to chambers and announced that it needed to go back because the gearbox was faulty. The clerks enquired what was wrong and he said, "it works fine in Day mode, just won't go anywhere in Night mode".

Another car story is a Q.C. at my chambers in Gray's Inn went out and bought a Bentley the day the conservatives (Nigel Lawson was the Chancellor of the Exchequer) changed the tax code for high earners. He arrived in chambers with a brand-new Bentley, walked into the clerks room and announced, "I'm calling it Nigel".

While at chambers in Manchester, a well-known Q.C. got kitted up for his 'Q.C. call day', tights, britches, silk gown and jumped in his car to get to the ceremony. Being late, he was pushed for time and attempted to take a short cut in his brand new, expensive car. Through the motorway services, out through the service road and just followed the lorry in front. As he was going through the barrier, the bollards came up under the car and completely lifted the car up in the air, writing it off at the same time. Now imagine a 60-year-old man, standing beside a wrecked expensive car, wearing tights, britches, and silk. "You see officer, I was late and on my way to …"

And finally, a story of a Ferrari … A barrister in Lincoln's Inn once failed to pay his clerk the fees he owed him (it was traditional in the old days for Barristers to pay the senior clerk directly the agreed percentage of his income, but that tradition has mainly been replaced by senior clerks on salaries these days).

The clerk had words with the barrister and the barrister simply said he could not afford to pay the clerk. The barrister said he had a few old cars in his garage and would the clerk take payment of the overdue fees by way of a car. The clerk went to the barrister's home and there in the garage was an old Ferrari looking a bit sad but still, it was a Ferrari. The clerk took the car rather than about £2,000 of fees. It was some time ago so that was quite a bit of money, even then.

The clerk sorted the car out, did a bit of restoration and enjoyed it for a few years before deciding to replace it. When he obtained a valuation, he was told it was worth £75,000! So, the unpaid fee turned out to be a good investment.

An amusing memory

I used to clerk a barrister called Edward Counsell who is still in practice in Bristol.

Mr Counsell used to do quite a lot of work for Somerset County Council at the time so he would introduce himself to the judge as, "Mr Counsell, of Counsel, acting on behalf of the Council." I always found that quite amusing.

Clerks room banter

Barrister; "Norman, a new sign on the lavatory door in the robing room 'Please do not place cigarette stubs in the toilets' can you have a word?"

Clerk responds; "Of course Sir, yes, it does make it difficult to pick them out and smoke them!"

Pupils

My story is about a pupil while I was at 3 Serjeants Inn, a London set of chambers (my second job) and I was a Junior Clerk in a specialist clinical negligence set of chambers. I was asked to make some teas and coffees for a senior member of chambers who was in the conference room with his solicitor and client. As I waited for the kettle to boil, one of our pupils asked me if she could help by making the tea for me. She knew I was busy, it was the afternoon and the courts had all started to produce their lists[13] and it was my job to check them against our list of cases and put the details in the diary. Surprised by this offer as no barrister had ever asked to help me before, I duly accepted the offer and went back to my desk to start checking the next day's lists.

---

[13] Lists are what each court produces each day to this day, showing the case order and judge for the next day's events. Every court in England and Wales produces a list and the listing officer is responsible for making sure that the cases are before the judges suitable for each type of case and they book more work than time available (a bit like airlines) because quite a few cases settle, meaning they do not need to go before the judge after all.

Twenty minutes later my phone rang and it was the barrister in the meeting room, "Where is my tea". Apology accepted that I had completely forgotten I went to the kitchen to find the pupil barrister staring at the kettle and asking me what she should do. She explained, "I have boiled the kettle, put the tea bags in, now what?". The kettle was a write off, I made a quick trip to the senior clerk, petty cash issued, ran to Robert Dyas where you could, and still can, buy just about everything, tea made and delivered to the barrister who just growled at me.

Where are my shoes?

One morning at South Western Chambers in Taunton I arrived early to do some criminal Legal Aid billing which was an ongoing and tedious task. It normally meant early mornings or weekends as it is just too busy during normal office hours when the barristers are in chambers.

It takes up to two hours for all of them to come in and say good morning, how are you, have you done this and that, then they go up to their rooms, the last one arriving about 10.30am and wanting to have a 'chat' with the clerk. Once all of them have asked you why you have not had a chance to do whatever it was they asked you to do the night before at 9pm when they left, you get that magic hour to yourself when you can do some work. That is before the early ones come down through the clerks room and inform you they are going for a long lunch with Mr X from Y's firm of solicitors. They kindly remind you that you have not done what they asked before and appear slightly baffled as to what we have been up to. By 1.30pm they have all gone out for lunch or asked us to go and get them a sandwich as they are really busy. Then the early ones come back from a shorter lunch, call in to make sure we are all okay and have a quick chat, then it is 3pm. The same process starts about 5pm when they go off to the pub or home to their families and by 7pm most of them have gone. Now we get some time to do the things we need to do so it is 9pm before you can think about going home.

Anyway, early this one specific Monday morning, Brian Lett called me on my mobile at 8am to say he was in a bit of a difficulty and I needed to help him. He had driven from Somerset to Kingston upon Thames late Sunday to be ready for his trial at Kingston upon Thames Crown Court the next day. Having driven up in his trainers, he realized on Monday morning at 8 o'clock he had no formal court shoes and was in a bit of a spin. I said don't worry, I would sort it and put the phone down.

My search of the Yellow Pages (as that was what you did then) came up with a Clarks shoe shop, directly opposite the court building so I called them. I think the lady who answered at 8.15am before the shop was open was a bit surprised by the caller from Somerset asking for a pair of black brogues, size 11 to be delivered to the security office of the court at 8.30am for collection by a barrister. I added £10 to the cost for her help and she took them over, duly deposited them at the security office just as Brian Lett walked up to the desk and was presented by the security guard with a new pair of shoes. The security guard thought it was hilarious, Brian Lett was just baffled and called me to say: "How the hell did you manage to do that?".

I'd like to say this situation is rare, but it is not. Clerks need to be masters of logistics as well as many other things.

Midnight mowing

The same Barrister, Brian Lett, once came into chambers and told me he thought he had upset his neighbour. Brian had quite a large farm type property on the outskirts of Taunton with a lot of grass to mow.

One day he was due to travel to Spain with his wife and family and the court hearing overran, as they quite often do, particularly when it was a lengthy and complex criminal trial which was Brian's speciality. On this particular day, the hearing went on for a few more days than expected so his wife and kids flew out to Spain and Brian would follow soon after.

The trial eventually ended and Brian re-booked himself a flight from Bristol but it was not until about 5am. Looking at his lawn and feeling it would not get cut again until after his return he decided the only thing to do was to get the lawn tractor out and start mowing. Having had a hard day in court he also fancied a glass of wine. He told me that he was not going to bed, just straight onto Bristol Airport by taxi at 3am so he did not bother to change from his pinstripe suit he wears in court under his robes. So Brian rode his tractor up and down his field at 1am, glass of wine in one hand, bottle of red in the other, wearing his suit and tie and was totally amazed that his neighbour came to have a go at him over the fence. I think he said the neighbour asked politely something like; "What the hell are you doing?" to which Brian simply replied; "Mowing my grass. Why?"

Barristers! Who would clerk them!

Before the arrival of the electronic diary, a Q.C. calls his clerk just after midnight, having just got in from a drinks party, wakes his clerk up from a deep sleep and says; "I want to go on holiday next week, what's in my diary?"

Clerk; "Sir, it's just gone midnight, I was fast asleep, and the diary is in chambers so I'll need to check".

Barrister; "Let me know as soon as you can".

Clerk arrives in chambers at 4.30am, checks the diary and calls barrister – "Who the b***** hell is calling me at this time in the morning!!!"

The lift incident

Atkin Chambers had a lift, quite an unusual feature of a building in the Inns which are historically old and listed. Atkin Chambers was a new building, added to the end of Raymond Buildings which was old and more traditional. Having a lift meant that someone had to have emergency training for lift evacuation and other strange things like how to open the doors when there was a power cut. As a junior clerk, this was my duty, so I had the training.

One day, I was carrying a huge pile of papers up to the third floor when the covering letter slipped off my pile and as it fell to the floor, went right down between the lift and the lift door in the smallest of gaps.

The letter was very important and had gone right down the lift shaft and was now laying in the pit at the bottom. My training kicked in, I fetched the lift keys, turned off the power, opened the doors at basement level, climbed down the ladder in the lift shaft, retrieved the offending letter and climbed back up, closed the basement doors and walked back up the stairs to the ground floor where the clerks room was. The lift doors were wide open, power off and lights off.

What I did not know, as I'd never actually turned off a lift before, was that the hydraulics were off and the lift was slowly sinking. It had sunk about three feet. The doors were wide open, the lift had sunk and a group of Barristers returned from lunch, perhaps after a wine or two, and walked right into the lift without looking. They fell about three feet with an almighty crash and ended up in a pile on the floor of the lift. Oops!

The pet shop joke

A barrister walked into a pet shop and was looking at the animals on display. While he was there, another barrister walked in and said to the shopkeeper; "I'll have a junior barristers' clerk monkey please." The shopkeeper nodded, went over to a cage full of monkeys and took out a monkey. He fitted a collar and leash, handed it to the barrister, saying, "That'll be £10,000." The barrister paid and walked out with his monkey.

Startled, the barrister went over to the shopkeeper and said; "That was a very expensive monkey. Most of them are only a few hundred pounds. Why did it cost so much?" The shopkeeper answered; "Ah, that monkey can take the barristers' books and papers to court very quickly, do the post and DX[14] accurately, answer the phone and make the tea, well worth the money."

---

[14] The DX, originally called the Document Exchange, was established in 1975 during the Royal Mail strikes of the seventies. It quickly became the preferred document delivery service for the legal sector. It is now widely used by the public and professional service companies including banks, police forces and courts. It started with one hub in London Chancery Lane. There are currently 35 sorting offices nationwide with 2,800 drop-off points.

The barrister looked at the *monkeys* in another cage: "They're even more expensive! £35,000! What do they do?"

"Oh, they're first junior clerk monkeys; they can answer all the barristers' questions, agree fees, book hearing dates in the diary, bill fees for work done, chase fees for work done, draft complicated letters, and chat up all the barristers' clients. All the difficult, really useful stuff," said the shopkeeper.

The barrister looked around for a little longer and saw a third monkey all by itself in a cage of its own, eating a banana. The price tag around its neck read £200,000. He gasped; "That one costs more than all the others put together! What on earth does it do?"

The shopkeeper replied; "Well, I haven't actually seen it do anything yet, but it says it's a Senior Clerk."

The missing barrister

The solicitor and clients are sitting in the waiting room in chambers waiting for a very senior member of chambers to arrive for the consultation.[15] Fifteen minutes later and the solicitor asks politely if we know how long Mr Smythe Q.C. might be.

We call his home which is at least 30 mins drive away and he answers. We advise him that his clients and solicitor are in the waiting room and he starts to explain his predicament: "We have no power, the car is in the garage, I have no idea how to get it out". The senior clerk explains that most electric garage doors will have a manual handle to one side and you can open the door.

Help provided, the clerk hangs up, advises the clients Mr Smythe Q.C. is half an hour away, offers more tea to placate an annoyed instructing solicitor and returns to desk.

Fifteen minutes later, the senior clerk's phone rings again and it is Mr Smythe Q.C. asking if the senior clerk could assist with how he opens his electric gates.

---

[15] Consultation is the word used for a meeting with a Q.C., it is a conference if it is a junior Barrister. i.e. not a Q.C. or pupil.

The sandwich

Junior clerks up and down the country pop to the local sandwich bars every day to buy sandwiches for busy barristers, it's what you do as "The Boy".

On this particular day we had a new boy and he was learning, only having been in the job a few days. The barrister asked the new boy to go and buy a sandwich and handed him a £20 note, adding: "And please do get something for yourself". The boy returned with the requested sandwich, handed it over and walked off. The barrister calling him back and asking for his change as he had given him a £20 note. The boy just explained that there was no change.

Confused the barrister said: "But it was a £20 note I gave you."

The boy replied: "You said to get something for myself, I bought a jumper".

The Barrister could not say anything so just walked off.

Updated guidance issued to the boy about how this all works and job done.

Image by Loren Conner

On another occasion, in a different chambers, a barrister asked the boy to go and get him a sandwich and when asked, "what would you like sir?" he replied: "Chicken, Egg, Ham, Tuna, Beef, whatever they have. The boy returned with a huge Scoobie snack and handed it over.

"Blimey, what's in this?" asked the barrister, the reply was, you guessed it ... "Chicken, Egg, Ham, Tuna, Beef".

Image by Loren Conner

You are sacked

In the old days it was normal for a small chambers to have just two clerks, a senior clerk and a junior clerk.

I recall being told of a call that came into Pump Court in the Temple one day from an angry solicitor. The senior clerk listened to a rant from a very important solicitor at a major London firm for ages but was getting a bit fed up as it seemed to be going on forever. Basically, the solicitor was upset that he had called earlier, spoken to the junior clerk called Tom and the message had not been passed onto the senior clerk. Fine, that is a perfectly acceptable complaint but the tirade was never going to stop.

The quick thinking senior clerk stopped the solicitor's moaning in his tracks, put the phone on the desk (not on hold) and gestured to the junior clerk to just sit still and not say a word, then he said to the junior clerk, very loudly so the solicitor on the phone could hear: "Now Tom, I have Mr Such and Such from such and such and company on the phone, he's really not happy as you have not passed on his important message to me. To be honest Tom, this is not the first time this has happened and I am pretty fed up with it now. We could lose business from Mr Such and Such and that is not acceptable," all the time gesturing to Tom to sit still, and ignore what he was saying. He went on to say: "Frankly, I've had enough, you are fired, get out, take your things and go, that's it, don't ever come back, you are sacked". Waving at the junior to stay seated and just stay silent, the senior clerk picked up the phone, spoke to Mr Such and Such and said: "Thank you for raising this with me, I have now dealt with it. You are right, it is unacceptable and I've sacked him". The call ended and the senior clerk looked at Tom and said: "Tom, you are now called Bob". Job done, all sorted.

A call to Dublin

One of our barristers needed a meeting in Dublin with a client and asked us to arrange somewhere to meet in central Dublin. Someone suggested we call Mr. O'Leary at a firm in Dublin as they had rooms and might allow us to use one.

We called the firm and a nice lady answered the phone and we asked to speak to Mr. O'Leary. The lady receptionist said: "Do you know which Mr. O'Leary it is you wish to speak to? Mr. O'Leary senior or Mr. O'Leary junior." We said sorry, we had no idea, we just wanted to ask about using a meeting room. She went on to say: "It's just that Mr. O'Leary senior passed away recently" ... so we spoke to Mr. O'Leary junior.

From Brian Lett Q.C. – Robing room banter

During a murder trial at the Old Bailey some years ago, the officer in charge of the investigation was a Detective Sergeant Livingstone. The challenge from my colleagues was to use the phrase in cross examination: "Dr Livingstone I presume." I won the challenge when cross-examining a different officer with the question: "Who called the doctor? Livingstone I presume." Happily, the jury got the joke!!

Excuse me sir!

It was 1985, and Motorola launched the new, latest mobile phone, I was working at Atkin Chambers and they were the proud owners of this new, fancy device. (The first ever call made on a mobile phone was 3 April 1973 by Martin Cooper, an employee at Motorola. He called Bell Labs, their main rivals, to say he was calling from his mobile phone).

I was dispatched to the Court of Appeal to collect some of our barristers who were appearing in a huge case. I was instructed to take the mobile telephone with me in case chambers needed me to do any other errands whilst away from chambers.

Pushing a trolley full of files and books meant that it was almost impossible to carry the mobile phone easily. I put the phone in a carrier bag and set off.

I was early for court which normally rises at 4.15pm each day so I sat in the back of the court, silently awaiting the familiar sound of 'court rise' from the usher that signalled the end of the court day. Everyone would stand up, bow to the judge and then when the judge had left the court, the barristers, solicitors, lay clients and witnesses etc could all sort out their papers and leave court.

On this occasion, I was rather shocked to realise the judge was talking to me and the court had gone silent. Being the Court of Appeal, there were three judges that day and one was talking directly to me. I was terrified (remember I was only 17), not just because of what he might say but what my Barristers would also say to my senior clerk later. The judge said: "Excuse me, your carrier bag appears to be ringing". I had no idea how to turn the phone off, answer it or anything else so I ran out of court rather quickly. Thankfully, everyone found it quite amusing but if that happened now, you could end up in the cells for contempt of court.

Fire alarm in chambers

A barrister (Q.C.) called me at 7.30 am to say they were in chambers, the fire alarm is going off, the building is full of smoke. He asked: "Should I leave a note for Wendy?"

Image by Loren Conner

Can I have some coffee please?

My colleague and I were in chambers in Gray's Inn late one evening and a Q.C. called up from the conference room and asked for some coffees. We were already late leaving and really wanted to catch our trains but not wishing to upset the Q.C., who was teaching about 50 law students the finer details of construction law, my colleague got the tea trolley, turned on the urn and duly made 50 cups of coffee, set out the biscuits and wheeled them in.

The Q.C. looked a bit surprised, thanked him, handed him ten sheets of paper and asked him to copy them three times. Oh whoops, it was copies, not coffees.

Image by Lorren Conner

A spot of toilet humour!

The Phantom Crapper

Long before I arrived at Atkin Chambers, the incident of the phantom crapper occurred and it was one of those stories the clerks like to tell in the pub after one or two beers.

Somebody reported to the senior clerk that the toilet on the third floor had been left in a terrible state and something needed to be done. The senior clerk went to investigate and came back to the clerks room saying it was indeed in a terrible state and the cleaner would be needed.

This started to happen on a regular basis so the senior clerk announced one day it was to be his mission to catch the phantom crapper and establish who it was as the mystery was beginning to be the talk of the chambers.

The senior clerk moved himself to a room directly opposite the toilet, kept his door ajar and inspected the toilet after each visit until he had caught the phantom crapper in the act (a member of the legal profession!).

The Middle Temple plumber came to visit

Many chambers have long narrow corridors with rooms on either side and a clerks room at the end. Crown Office Row is one such chambers.

One day the Middle Temple plumber was called to unblock the toilet in chambers. All pretty normal. However, as the plumber stood in the doorway to the clerks room announcing that he had completed the work and the toilet was now flowing freely, one of the clerks, for reasons unknown to me to this day asked: "What was the problem?" to which the plumber, filling the entire doorway, began to provide a very graphic explanation.

The plumber was now causing a blockage of his own as the barristers who could not get into the clerks room were lined up behind the plumber, all anxious to get past. Undeterred the plumber began his explanation of what he had managed to achieve: "You see guys, there was the most f . . . . . g great curly turd stuck in the U-bend and I had to put my had right up there to push it onwards" gesturing that the offending curly turd was: "this wide." and holding his arms out about three foot apart. Behind him the barristers looked rather shocked, the clerks looked down at their desks and tried not to laugh.

Littlewoods Pools winner

While I was Senior Clerk at South Western Chambers in Taunton, we were asked to prosecute in a six-week car ringing case in Poole Crown Court by the regional special cases squad. Brian Lett (now a Q.C.) took on the case and everything went normally for the six weeks.

As the case was due to finish, I went along to court to do the usual clerking role of making sure the solicitor was happy with the service provided. I would possibly buy them a pint or two if the case was a success, or buy them a pint or two if they were commiserating – either way, the barristers and solicitors normally had a pint after a long trial.

I arrived at lunchtime and the judge said he would adjourn the trial over lunch and then deliver his sentence as the jury had already found the defendant guilty on most counts. The sentence was going to be a long one as it involved a lot of cars over a long period of time.

We came back from lunch, were just about ready to go when a chap walked into the court room asking if he could speak to the defendant. The judge said this was highly irregular but was intrigued to know what was going on. The chap went to the dock and passed the defendant a letter informing him he had won £1m on the pools and shook his hand. The judge asked to look at the letter and that was that.

The judge delivered his sentence of a lengthy prison sentence and asked the defendant if he wanted to say anything. He looked at the judge and just said: "I'd like to sack my barrister", which he did. The barrister left court.

I tapped the CPS representative on the shoulder, asked if we could have a quick word outside. I asked if we could negotiate the fee there and then, which was highly unusual, so Brian Lett could ask for a costs order against the defendant. The fee was agreed and a costs order was secured which saved the CPS quite a bit of money for a six-week trial as costs orders are not made that often – defendants do not tend to have the means to pay as they go off to prison. The judge informed the defendant of the amount of the costs he would have to pay, then asked again if he had anything further to say and he just replied: "Is that all? Can I go now?"

The next day, *The Sun* newspaper printed a headline and inside a cartoon of the defendant, in his prison clothes, sitting in a cell with a prison officer serving his dinner from a silver service set.

What day of the week is it?

Two Crown Office Row many years ago – a Q.C. walked into the clerks room and asked the entire room what day of the week it was. Before anyone could speak, he announced: "Oh, it's Monday of course, how silly of me". We laughed and carried on with our work until five minutes later he walked back in and declared: "How silly of me, I'm really embarrassed, it's Wednesday," and walked off again. We laughed again ... it was a Tuesday!

Michael Jackson and Tom Jones

It was Christmas Eve, everyone had gone to the pub, I was the loner left in chambers to man the ship, just in case someone should call, which they wouldn't, but I was left in charge, I was responsible. I could leave at 5pm and meet the others in the pub, that was the deal.

At 3pm, the phone rings, it is a clerk from 3 Hare Court, John Grimmer, we will call him that because that is his name. He said that he was stuck, he needed a barrister to represent their client Michael Jackson at Horseferry Road Magistrates Court and could I sort it out quickly.

Well, John Grimmer is a good mate of my senior clerk, who is in the pub. I sense a wind up but I'm too junior to actually suggest that. I organise the barrister and despatch him to the Magistrates Court with a sincere apology saying I honestly feel I am wasting his time. junior barristers tend to do what the clerks ask, give a smile and trot off.

Five minutes later we have another client who needs urgent representation at the same court, could I help. No problem I say, fully aware it is Christmas Eve and why not go along with the flow. His name is 'Tom Jones' says the clerk asking for help. No problem I reply, we are on it. I agreed with the barrister that I would buy the beer when he comes back from his wasted trip later today.

At 6pm we are in the Deveraux Pub just by the Fountain Court Gate from Temple (now sadly closed and destined to become flats, it seems lawyers don't drink as much these days which I find hard to believe), the barrister returns looking a bit fed up, allowed me to pay for three to four pints before he could hold his poker face no longer and broke into laughter that in fact he had looked after two clients that afternoon, a Mr. Michael Jackson and a Mr. Tom Jones. True story!

The boob in the soup

I was a junior clerk, nervous of the chambers Christmas party but this year was different, I had recently become engaged so I had my fiancé to take to the party. She was equally nervous about the dress code and eating with 50 senior barristers. However, she was not prepared for what actually happened.

We sat on a table of 10 or so, the soup starter was served (tomato if I remember correctly) and the lady wife of a senior Q.C., part-time judge

Image by Loren Conner

84

in the Technology and Construction court, was pretty smashed before we started. I am using that phrased deliberately as she was completely smashed. She was wearing one of those dresses that your boobs just sat in, nothing apparently keeping them safe. Claire was surprised to say the least but we did our best to keep polite conversation going and do the right thing, whatever that is. Then it happened, the Q.C.'s wife leant forward to reach out for the bread basket and the left boob just plopped into the soup. My fiancé and I froze, looked a bit shocked and did our best to work out what you do in that situation. The wife on the other hand was mid conversation with someone so she picked it up, wiped it with her napkin and popped it back in without even a slight change of expression.

Help me with my aged debt old boy!

Stanley Best arrived at chambers one day and asked one of the clerks if he could help him with his aged debt. "Yes," said the clerk, "what would you like me to do?" He replied, "It's in my boot, it needs to come into chambers."

This is the same barrister who once put in a time sheet to be billed on the old Legal Aid rates for public work and put travel down from Barnstaple to a prison in Norwich as 27 hours. We queried it and asked for the correct figure. He came back to us and said it was correct, just bill it. When we asked how it could possibly take 27 hours to Norwich from Barnstaple, he said that he did not like to take his mini metro on the motorway.

I was once away for the weekend in Barnstaple with my wife and noticed Stanley coming out of a shop with his newspaper. I was about to say hello as he got into his red mini metro when all of a sudden a man came running down the road shouting at him and gesturing in a frenzied manor. I stayed well clear and tried to work out what chaos Stanley was causing in Barnstaple that day. It turned out, Stanley's red mini metro was parked about four cars back and this was an identical one. The chap simply could not understand why this elderly man was sitting in his car trying to start it. I sunk into the background so Stanley has no idea I witnessed that event.

Two boating stories

Call the Coastguard

You will no doubt have gathered clerks often get asked questions which can be out of the ordinary. I think this one comes under that category.

We once had a barrister who told us he was thinking of buying a boat. "Nothing glamorous and I won't be going too far," he said, "Just an old rust bucket I can potter around the coast in when I feel like it". Sure enough, one day I took a call from him when he told me he was now the proud owner of an old tub and he was feeling quite the master mariner as he pottered around the coast.

I thought no more of this until a few days later I received another call from him, this time in a rather panicked voice: "Um. I'm on the boat again but I've run into a spot of bother. Turns out there's a sandbar here and I'm a bit stuck. Can you google the Coastguard for me and tell me the number?" A few minutes later: "Could you call the coastguard for me"? I asked, "Which coastguard? Where are you"? The reply was, "Dunno".

Image by Loren Conner

Another boat tale

A member of chambers who lived along the Thames had just brought a new boat and wanted to put it to good use. So, one morning the clerks room received a call saying he would be collecting his papers for the next day using his new toy. The papers were wrapped in a couple of plastic bags and lots of Sellotape to allow them to be thrown to him from the Embankment. At the allotted time in the afternoon one of the junior clerks was despatched to the Embankment to wait for his arrival. About an hour later we received a call (no mobile phones as this was in the 1980s) from the said barrister saying the rope was tangled around the propeller and he was not going to make it. So, another junior clerk was sent to bring the first one back to chambers and the papers re-packaged and taken to Waterloo Red Star office to be delivered in the normal way.

The Yanks are coming to visit

A Judge from Texas arrived in chambers, and as he was walking down the corridor Tom was on the phone to a difficult solicitor. In those days you were allowed to smoke indoors and Tom did. He had also perfected the act of lighting his cigarette, using a match and one handedly sending the match cross the room and into the bin!

On this particular day the match did not go out and landing in the bin setting fire to the contents. Flames started to appear over the top of the bin which caused the rest of the clerks room to burst into laughter and a panicked look to appear on Tom's face. He stood while still speaking on the phone and moved over to the bin and started to try to put out the fire! By this stage the Judge had made his way down the corridor and was standing in the doorway. Tom with his feet in the bin and the rest of us trying not to laugh as the Judge announced: "Gee Quintin* told me I would get a warm welcome in London but I didn't expect it to be this warm!"

(*Quintin Edwards Q.C. was a member of 2COR before becoming a Circuit Judge.)

The tale of a new overcoat

The senior clerk in a very prestigious commercial chambers was visited in his room one day by a newly appointed Silk who asked him: "I have just bought myself this new overcoat and wanted to know what you thought of it?" The senior clerk replied, peering over the top of his glasses: "No, I don't like that at all. I don't think it befits someone of your stature and I would not want to see you wearing it around the Temple again". The Silk replied: "Well, I rather like it," to which the clerk replied: "You have asked for my opinion and now you have it".

The following day, the Silk came in to chambers again wearing his new overcoat and left it in chambers while he went for lunch at the Inn. After coming back from lunch, he rushed into the senior clerks room and said: "I've just come back from lunch and my brand-new overcoat is cut up in pieces and has been left in a plastic bag on top of my desk!". The senior clerk replied: "Yes, you came to see me yesterday and asked me for my opinion, and frankly I hoped that you would have accepted it. Now, I think you should take yourself off to Gieves & Hawkes in Saville Row where they make coats for gentlemen, far more befitting someone of your stature. Get yourself something made and have them put it on my account!".

Apparently the Silk, though crest fallen, accepted this!

CPS regular meetings with chambers

Some years ago the CPS had agreements with chambers in London who worked for them that they would have regular meetings to assess and discuss chambers performance and how things could be improved for the benefit of chambers and the CPS.

At one of these meetings with a senior clerk in London, the meeting followed its usual format and at the end the CPS representatives informed the clerk that they had a bit of a sensitive issue to deal with. They said that they had had some complaints from CPS staff about one of his barristers and that as there were several complaints the decision had been made that the CPS were no longer prepared to instruct him. The clerk said he was very disturbed and sorry to hear that and asked which barrister they were referring to? When they gave him the name, the clerk replied: "Well actually that's not going to be an issue as he has now left chambers". The CPS representative replied: "Okay but we had better make a note of which chambers he has gone to so that we don't instruct him at that set either". The clerk replied: "He hasn't gone to another set, he has joined the CPS as a Crown Court Advocate!"

Late to court

On the morning of the 7/7 attacks in London when of course there was huge travel disruption across London and many barristers either could not make it to court at all or were severely delayed, one clerk received a call from Woolwich Crown Court, which went as follows.

Court: "Hello I'm calling from Woolwich Crown Court and I understand that your Mr. X is due to be prosecuting a case in Court 1 at 10.00. It is now 10.15 and he has not arrived, can you let me know why that is and when he will arrive?"

Clerk: "He has been caught up in all of the travel disruption which you may have heard about and is doing his best to get there as soon as he can".

Court: "That is not acceptable as everyone else is here and ready for the case to go ahead".

Clerk: "That is unfortunate but I can assure you he is doing everything he can to get there and if the judge is not happy about it then frankly he can go and f**k himself".

Court: "I am the judge".

Thanks to Tim Markham for that one.

The blackboard at Wolverhampton Crown Court

A member of chambers was conducting a month's fraud trial in Wolverhampton which revolved around a warehouse fire. A lot of the evidence centred on the financial state of the company.

I arrived to have breakfast with counsel and the instructing solicitor in the second week of the trial, to be told that the accountant for the prosecution had filled two sides of a blackboard with rather damming evidence against the four defendants the previous day. An enjoyable breakfast was had and we made our way to court for the cross examination of the accountant.

All rise and the Judge entered, and the day's processing got under way.

Defence Counsel rises and states: "Members of the jury may I take you back to your school days, there was always one teacher's pet who was asked to do various jobs around the classroom including cleaning the blackboard. I was never that child but sometime wished I was."

With that he left counsels' row walking round the front of the court, passed the jury and the Judge, got to the blackboard and picked up a cloth and starting cleaning it, much to the amusement of all those in court. Returning to his seat he turned to his instructing solicitors and said: "That is one side cleared now how do we clear the other."

Dressing for court

In the days when barristers wore pinstriped trousers to court and clerks accompanied Silks to court, on the first day of a murder trial Q.C.s were expected to wear their silk robe, court jacket and waistcoat and not their stuffed gown (material the gown is made from) and bum freezer which are so popular now.

A clerk was told the following day he was to go to Winchester Crown Court to take the Silk's papers (yes papers) and robes, deliver them to the robing room and help the Q.C. dress. The evening before the senior clerk had given him instruction and a demonstration on how to assist with the dressing.

The following day on arriving at the court accompanied by the other side's clerk they made their way to robing room to be greeted by their Silks. Off comes the Silk's jacket while the clerk opened his suitcase, next went his collar and bands. While the Silk is adjusting his collar the clerk took out his waistcoat and held it up behind him for him to slip his arms into. However, the Silk had other ideas and dropped his trousers to the floor much to the surprise and amazement of the clerk (this had not been part of the demo!!). The Silk turned his head and said: "Trousers first boy, trousers first," to which the clerk fumbled in the suitcase to find a pair of pinstriped trousers.

Falling asleep on the train

In the days before mobile phones a member of chambers came up to London to go to the Court of Appeal. The case went short so he decided to take his clerk for a 'proper' lunch. Lunch ran into the evening and a good time was had by both.

He got the last train from London to a small station just outside Southampton. The train was empty so he took his shoes off, put his feet on the seat opposite and went to sleep. Waking with a start, he found he had passed his stop and was at the next, even quieter station. He grabbed his bag and leapt off the train. As the train pulled out he realised that his shoes were still on-board.

The evening got worse as the station had no minicab office and the phone box had been vandalised. After a long walk of just under four miles with no shoes, he then had the pleasure of explaining everything to his wife!

The Old Bailey

One day I took the papers for a barrister to the Old Bailey, just down Fleet Street and up from Ludgate Circus. The case started as normal with the call of 'All rise' from the usher.

As a clerk, you wait five or ten minutes to make sure the barrister is all right and nothing has been left in chambers before you leave.

On this particular day, Geoffrey Conlin realised he had not been to the toilet and the next break would be lunch if not before. He rose up, signalled to the judge he wanted to speak which rather irritated the judge, as it does. Mr Conlin explained that he had forgotten to go to the toilet and could he have a few minutes break. The judge then proceeded to give a five-minute lecture about the importance of going to the toilet and not wasting court time. He went on to say it costs thousands of pounds a minute to run the Old Bailey and he was not amused by Mr Conlin's request, to which Mr Conlin stood up and replied by saying: "Your Honour, I assure you I will only spend a penny". It is fair to say the judge was not amused.

Books to the Court of Appeal

Back in the days before photocopies were of the quality they are now and before the Internet, hard copy authorities were taken to court.

Our head of chambers was appearing in the Court of Appeal and had been preparing it for several days. The number of authorities, reported cases that he was going to rely on, grew and grew to around 50 (probably only 25 but they weighed a ton).

The day before the hearing I was given a list to deliver to the usher in Court 4 for the following day. The usher was none too pleased to see the length of the list and the fact she needed to find three copies of each, one for each of the Judges.

The morning of the hearing I strapped up the books and carried them, rather precariously, over to the High Court. On entering the court and setting all the books up, his opponent marched over to him and made reference to the number of authorities, to which my head of chambers stated: "I hope I will not be needing to refer to many of them". Much to the dismay of the usher and myself he used only one authority!! At least I had not dropped them on the zebra crossing!

Junior clerks

A junior clerk in Lincoln's Inn. It was a really busy morning in chambers, all the clerks hit the ground running as soon as they arrived. Like most days in chambers, no one could get out for lunch ... junior clerk was absolutely starving and asked the senior clerk if he could go into the kitchen to make himself some lunch ... senior clerk agreed, "but be quick" ... next thing you hear is ridiculously loud sizzling, popping, with smoke coming from underneath the kitchen door ... senior clerk bursts in to find the junior clerk cooking a full English breakfast (eggs, bacon, sausages and beans) on the coffee hot plate.

Thanks to Tony Stephenson for that one.

PART TWO
Propping up the bar

Frank Parsliffe

Barristers' Clerk 1936–1916 . . .
(except for four years during World War Two)
Frank died on 1 April 2016, he would have found it amusing that he
passed away on April Fool's Day.

Franks's wife and family have given permission to print Frank's manuscript. We have kept to the original text where possible but would ask that you bear in mind it was Frank's personal thoughts and written in a very different time.

CHAPTER ONE
It all started with Adam

"This old building doesn't look like it," I said.

"I think it is, Frank" said my mother. Look, his name is up on the wall! So it was with great trepidation that the two of us mounted the rickety staircase of the building called The Cloisters in the Temple, off Fleet Street.

The event was mid-afternoon one day in early October 1936. I was a very green fourteen and a half-year-old boy, about to take my first hesitant step in the big hectic world of working London. The purpose was an interview with a certain King's Counsel, hopefully to be accepted and employed as the 'boy' in that set of barristers' chambers.

Only hours earlier on the same day, I had been one of a class of pupils enjoying the routine of life in our last year at St. Bernard's Central School in the heart of Whitechapel. Although preparatory school at that time required leaving at the age of 14, the Central Schools allowed an extra year for extended training in commercial and technical subjects.

Being quite hopeless at anything technical, I had chosen the commercial side of the education available, a year or two before. Armed with a few Royal Society of Arts' Certificates, notably English, bookkeeping, shorthand and typewriting, I nurtured the hope of finishing up in a City office.

These awards, with or without 'Credit', were roughly the equivalent of the 'A' and 'O' levels of today. The Central School system was very good at using the fifteenth year for a bit of fine tuning before pointing their pupils in the right direction in the quest for an appropriate niche in life. On the October morning, my tranquil studies were interrupted abruptly by my headmaster, a very dour and portly Scot called McCann, who entered our classroom and told the teacher to release me at once. As we were not on the telephone, my mother had asked a near neighbour to go from our house in Bow some mile or two away, to fetch me as a matter of great urgency.

Mrs. Gore, normally a jolly and lively woman, was on this occasion most solemn and remained silent except to say that she could not tell me why I was needed at home.

During the bus ride home along the Mile End Road, I became more and more worried and was filled with the most terrible foreboding about death, fires, etc.

The fear grew to such an extent, that by the time we reached home, I was reconciled to a totally wiped out family, the victims of a 'titanic scale' disaster or something equally macabre. I was greeted by a radiantly happy mother who smilingly and excitedly announced that she had got me (or hoped she had got me) a job with Mr. Richard O'Sullivan K.C. We were to go up to the City soon after lunch for an interview.

I do not know to this day why my mother did not come to the school herself or pass a reassuring message not to worry with the neighbour. The fact is, although my fears were unfounded, I was still in a state of numb shock and accepted, without argument, what she had arranged. I doubt whether I had taken in fully what it was all about. Certainly I would normally have been sceptical about her accompanying me for the interview, but in the circumstances, it was a matter of no great import. The reason for my mother's over-zealous enthusiasm was because of her undying regard and admiration for Richard O'Sullivan. She was a devout Catholic and one of her religious and social highlights was to attend every second Sunday in the month at the Convent of the Little Sisters of the Assumption in Wellington Way, off Bow Road.

These charitable and compassionate nuns would invite guest speakers to the monthly mothers' meetings. By far the most popular and success-ful of these was the resident speaker, Richard O'Sullivan.

He would hold his audience spellbound with his Irish charm and charisma – regaling wondrous stories of life in the Emerald Isle. The impact on my mother was quite profound, although I think my non-

Catholic father (a London bobby) was not amused or impressed when she returned home after such meetings, quite starry eyed with an obvious feeling of spiritual well-being. Apparently Richard O'Sullivan had asked the Reverend Mother of the Convent if she knew of any local 'bright' boy and Mrs. Parsliffe's offspring was mentioned as a possibility. With no consultation of any kind and without delay I was presented as a candidate.

We arrived on the first floor of the building and gingerly knocked on the ancient door. After a few moments, it was opened by a thin, middle-aged, grey-haired man with a small Hitler-like moustache.

He was, I soon learned, called Adam and was the senior clerk, otherwise known as 'the Clerk to Chambers'. I also learned, not much later, that the moustache was not the only similarity with Hitler. He greeted us as if we had just crawled out from under a stone and commanded us to: "walk this way!" Crossing a very small dark hallway we were ushered surreptitiously into the room or chamber of the revered Richard O'Sullivan. This was the first time that I had met him.

He was, I guess, in his mid-forties, with great presence and looked a kindly and benign man with a happy grin. He thanked Adam more out of courtesy than genuine gratitude as he withdrew. The next half hour was taken up with the interviewer and my mother talking avidly about everything other than the purpose of our visit. I sat silently, holding my precious R.S.A.s, ready to produce them at a moment's notice, but it was not to be. Adam suddenly re-appeared and I was told to start work the following Monday at 9.00a.m. sharp! The fact that I had to request the school to approve and release me was not even referred to, nor was anyone apparently interested in whether I wanted the job or not!

This was probably the only occasion that I can recall my mother being so assertive. All that mattered was that Richard O'Sullivan was about to employ me. I vaguely remember reporting back to the head-master and that it met with his full approval, no doubt because the law and King's Counsel (now Queen's Counsel) had and still have a certain magic. In his mind it had to be good.

On the appointed day I arrived in a new suit just before 9.00a.m. at the chambers in The Cloisters. Adam was there with his assistant, Harold Goodale. With a rasping and prolonged "P-a-r-s-l-i-f-f-e, come here," he told me to call his assistant Mr. Goodale and himself 'Sir'. There was nothing reassuring like a: "Good morning" which would have helped. The clerks' room was an absurdly small area behind a glass partition, the other side of which was the dark hallway. This was also used as a waiting room although there were no tables or chairs. The whole environment, as well as being dark, was mean and depressing.

I was given about one square foot on the corner of the junior clerk's desk, which was only about four feet by two feet anyway, and which was pushed right into the corner.

On my share I had to perform any clerical chores flung my way, such as the post book and envelope addressing. In addition the main duties were such as telephone answering, book carrying, letter delivering, running numerous errands, fetching coal and my piece de resistance – making spills for the fires! The last named was soon revealed to me.

On my first day Adam said that if I found that I had nothing to do at any time I must use the time producing spills. I was instructed in how to wet my fingers and roll the sheets of the old *Times* newspapers, starting at one corner and making a tight long stick of paper before folding it over and over and tucking it in to produce an object about four inches long. They were extremely effective for lighting fires and saved the expense of buying wood.

In time, I became quite proficient at it and as I was urged to look busy at all time (you can always do a few more spills) quite a mountain of them were produced each day. These were piled up next to a ghastly old gas stove which gave of a toxic aroma and, as Adam would not allow any windows to be opened, whatever the climate outside, it is a wonder we survived with reasonable health or that the building was not raised to the ground by fire. (Later the real Hitler did just that in 1941). I once asked why we could not have the window open and got a ticking off for my pains.

I was concerned about my academic skills, such as they were, which were not called upon in the job and I therefore kept up with some of the training by going to night school. Adam could not really object to me going early two nights a week. I suspect my motives were not entirely educational but sprung from a desire to get away from the place. I regretted every moment of it.

Also I felt cheated, having been denied the chance to finish my schooling. I would gladly have given notice and taken my chance elsewhere, but for my mother's adulation of her hero, whose health and career she enquired about every night when I got home. Even that was embarrassing after a few weeks, as it became apparent to me that Richard O'Sullivan was not one of the most successful barristers and seldom appeared in Court. As I did not wish to dampen her enthusiasm I normally gave a non-committal reply.

There had been no mention at the interview of the salary and as it would have been unfitting in those days to enquire, I was depressed when I found that I was only paid twelve shillings and sixpence (62p) on the first pay day. This was considered, in 1936, to be the very bottom of the salary band. It would be another ten months or so before there was to be an increase – another one shilling and sixpence – making fourteen shillings (70p) a week! This was something of an insult as two shillings and sixpence was universally regarded as the minimum unit of increase, the progression being twelve shillings and sixpence, fifteen shillings – (sometimes seventeen shillings and sixpence), £1 thereafter; £1 and five shillings, £1 and ten shillings and so on.

Nine or ten of the barristers, all of whom were male, practised from The Cloisters. Although there were a handful of women at the bar, then notably Mrs. Eleanor Normanton – the first lady K.C., the prejudice against women in most sets of chambers was complete. This attitude prevailed until well after the war, but nowadays it can be said, I think, to be at a minimum.

Our chambers was typical of the format which existed then and, to some extent, up to the present day. Except in a few specialist sets there was no central planning as to balance. The component parts were barristers acting not in unison as in partnership, but almost entirely independently, relying on their own ability or the patronage of the clerk to feed them with work.

As there was too little to go round, the power and influence of the clerk was paramount. He it was, who on occasion, received requests from solicitors for appropriate counsel and he advised or allocated accordingly. So Adam was 'King!' Although unqualified as a lawyer, he had an ability to gain the trust of solicitors, albeit with a certain professional charm, even more than that of his employers, the barristers, who appeared to regard him with cold respect, but he ruled and survived!

There were two King's Counsel in chambers. The more senior and, as such, the Head of Chambers, was Mr. St. John Field. He was very affluent and stylish and did not need the patronage of Adam or the profession to survive. He, too, was not amongst the front runners at the Bar and was not often in Court. He was a very imposing figure, elegantly dressed in top hat, tails and spats and wore a monocle.

His daughter, Virginia Field, was a famous actress in Hollywood at the time, a very beautiful girl, who sent my pulse racing on the few occasions when she rang chambers and I answered the telephone. When not in court, Mr. Field usually arrived in chambers at about 11.00a.m., accompanied by his peak-capped chauffeur, carrying his briefcase up the staircase to the first floor. There Adam made it his business to be available to receive him and relieve the driver of the case. They then ascended to the second floor, where Mr. Field had his room, Adam engaging him in small talk, which I imagine his boss would have sooner had done without. He would then leave chambers at about 4.00p.m., accompanied by his faithful servant, unless he was in demand for any professional consultations.

Neither of the King's Counsel could boast a heavy practice, although Mr. Field was made a County Court Judge much later. Neither had the volume of work which some junior members of chambers enjoyed.

These included Mr. Harold Brown (later also a County Court Judge), Mr. Douglas Lowe (now a Q.C.,) and Mr. Reginald Paget (now Lord Paget of Northampton in the House of Lords). But none could match the astronomical success of Mr. Gerald Gardiner.

In 1936 Mr. Gardiner was only the third name up from the bottom of the list painted on the outside of the main door. This showed the order of seniority of each of the professionals housed as a group as 'a set of Chambers', based on the day of call to the appropriate Inn of Court. There were four – the Middle Temple, the Inner Temple, Lincoln's Inn and Gray's Inn. He already attracted almost as much work as the rest put together and was the main reason why I was engaged to carry books to and from the Law Courts. In the fullness of time he became a K.C.

When the much in demand Sir Hartley Shawcross K.C., retired to become a legal adviser to the Shell Petroleum Company, Gardiner took over as probably the most successful 'Silk' (K.C.) then at the Bar. He had a very busy practice and excelled in libel and slander cases of the time. He was particularly effective as a civil jury advocate with an extraordinary high success rate. Tall and thin, with a sallow complexion and impeccable manners, he epitomised the purist image of the best of the Bar. He was fastidious with his preparation, made copious notes and, when addressing judge or jury, presented his case with no vestige of hesitation or doubt of purpose.

I was also very impressed with his habit of immediately sitting down whenever his opponent, wisely or not, rose to object to anything Gerald Gardiner was saying. Nothing, in my view, could be more effective to show absolute confidence in one's case. But he was considered by many to be a very odd man, lacking the personality or showmanship normally attributed to other able jury advocates, such as Gilbert Beyfus Q.C., Gilbert Pauli Q.C., and above all, Shawcross.

His active interest in politics was minimal. I think he once stood as an unsuccessful Labour candidate many years ago in a London constituency – but it was enough to impress Harold Wilson when Labour beat Lord Home's administration by three votes in 1964. He immediately appointed Gerald Gardiner as his Lord Chancellor. This was a very rare achievement, going as he did, straight from the Bar to the Head of Judiciary without holding any of the intermediate legal offices.

All that was, of course, much later. Naturally I was too young at the beginning to appreciate that these exalted things would come to pass. All the more so because at our first encounter I perpetrated one of my gaffes. It came about in the following way: On the first day, after the instruction regarding firelights, I was taken by Harold Goodale on a five-minute walk and shown round the Law Courts. This was to be a brief introduction to what it was all about. At about 10.15a.m., we went the few yards, past the church, out of the Temple, and crossed the main road by the obelisk called Temple Bar – the point where the Strand and Fleet Street meet.

We entered the gothic museum-like building on the other side of the busy thoroughfare and into the inspiring Central Hall of the Royal Courts of Justice (to give the place its official title). My initial impression of its grandeur was that with its huge size and very high ceiling, had it been furnished with rows and rows of chairs and benches, and possessed a marble altar and pulpit, it could have been a cathedral.

Our tour included the two courts which concerned our principals on that day. Goodale explained to me how to lay out the appropriate books and papers (which I had been carrying) in the place reserved for them on the benches. Leading Counsel, when appearing in Court, occupied the front row facing the judge. Juniors sit behind their seniors in the second pew whilst solicitors, clients and witnesses are allowed in the third within easy access of the advocates. As an alternative, the latter group can use a small table just in front of, but lower than, the silk. This, however, rarely seems to be sufficiently large enough for their purposes.

Once the court is in session no-one else is allowed in the first two pews. Any clerking duties have to be performed before the judge takes his place high up on the bench.

Not knowing this I was soon to suffer a most traumatic experience. It occurred in the Lord Chief Justice of England's court, one of the two we were to visit. This is by far the largest and the only one with a centre aisle separating the antagonists. The opposing silks usually sit not far from each other on either side of this division, some way from the outside entrances to their row. Sir Patrick Hastings was the K.C. on this occasion and behind him was his junior, the imposing Gerald Gardiner.

Standing to one side, along with the other clerks, I was, firstly, overtaken by a feeling of great awe as everyone rose and bowed to the diminutive figure of Lord Chief Justice Hewitt as he took his seat. He looked like a very hostile owl. I felt that I was on trial so solemn did the proceedings seem.

I must confess I was pleased a few minutes later to get out into the fresh air, having been sent back to the Cloisters by Harold. My sense of relief was soon dispelled. I had hardly arrived when Adam handed me a thin batch of papers, tied up by pink ribbon, and I was curtly told to get back urgently from whence I had come. My orders were to ask Mr. Goodale to pass the bundle, which apparently related to the existing case, to Mr. Gardiner. "You saw him this morning, he is the tall slim one," said Adam. He went on: "You know which court he's in – off you go and be quick about it".

I made my way back but discovered to my horror and with a growing sense of panic and nausea that Harold Goodale had moved on to his other duties – I knew not where. For a moment or two I did not know what to do. Then, realising that this was an opportunity for me to display my initiative, there was nothing for it but to pass the papers myself. But how was that to be done? One immediate difficulty was that there were a number of wigged and gowned junior barristers occupying the second row between where I stood and Mr. Gardiner, who was clearly fully engrossed in his work. So that avenue was blocked, and, as there were quite a few clients and witnesses seated, so was the third row. Then I saw the answer. As Sir Patrick was the only person in the front bench I could approach by that means and hand the papers over his shoulder to my boss behind. Taking a deep breath I stealthily stalked the few yards along the row, apologising to all concerned, including Sir Patrick. Gerald Gardiner looked up long enough only to nod his thanks as he took the papers from me.

Just at that moment I thought my end had come. I was suddenly and expertly seized by no less than the three ushers usually on duty in that court. I was physically lifted up, bundled out silently but quite swiftly and deposited through the door in the corridor outside, not unlike an intruder to an exclusive club getting the treatment from the tough bouncers. One of them allowed himself the chance of delivering a well worded admonishment: "Don't you ever do that again, boy. If you do, you really will get my boot up your arse. You must thank your lucky stars, the Lord Chief didn't see you!"

The whole operation had taken, I would guess, about five seconds. Totally stunned, I wended my weary way back to chambers. The day was not going at all well. About the only thing I did right was in not reporting the incident to Adam. I believe Harold probably heard about it later but, thankfully, kept it to himself. The mind boggles when I mull over the consequences had 'Hitler' been informed. One thing was certain – never again, even in an otherwise empty court, would I enter the silks' row without a shudder. I suppose this was one of the most sure ways of learning 'what it was all about'.

Only once do I recall Adam showing any sign of charity. I was expected to work every Saturday morning until about 12.30 whereas he and Harold Goodale alternated working on that day. On one particular Saturday morning, when it was the senior clerk's turn, there was the need for a parcel containing a brief to be taken to Euston for urgent despatch to the north. Adam said (and this was the cherished moment): "You can take a cab if you wish".

The prospect of charging for a cab but going by Underground leaving a fair residue of cash in my favour filled me with great joy. Thanking him, I raced off with the parcel and the ten-shilling note (fifty pence) produced from the petty cash tin.

The fare to and from Euston was about 3d each way (a shade over one pence) by Underground. After disposing of the parcel, I approached a taxi driver at the head of the rank at the main line station and enquired how much it would cost for a cab to the Temple off Fleet Street? After an unpleasant series of questions such as: "Are you hiring this bloody cab or aren't you?" I elicited the good news that it would cost about 3/3d (three shillings and three pence old money) for a single trip.

Thanking him for his courtesy, I took the Tube back, happily working out my gains. With the parcel at 2/9d (two shillings and nine pence – old money) plus two times 3/3d for the cab, (a total of nine shillings and three pence) the change due to Adam was 9d, leaving me with a profit of 6/- (thirty pence). This represented nearly half a week's salary. I did not feel quite like Rothschild with his first million, but I began to have a sense of financial security. Alas the euphoria was short lived. On returning to Chambers and proffering the 9d to Adam, I was subjected to a severe reprimand: "I only meant one way, you silly boy," he said and demanded the return of the 3/-, thereby halving the ill-gotten reward for my labours.

I now had been in the job for nearly fourteen months and there seemed to be no great promise for the future. The time was rapidly approaching when I would have to leave as Adam was getting me down. He seemed to have a natural aptitude to be as distasteful as possible to his subordinates. Even Harold Goodale had adopted a rather numb acceptance of his role.

Many years later after the war he and I, despite our ten years' difference in age, were to become extremely close friends. I was not surprised when he informed me that no boy had lasted more than four or five weeks in the Cloisters' job. Either they were sacked or they could not stand the strain. I finally informed my mother that all was not well. I believe she had guessed as much as mothers instinctively do. I had not reacted warmly to her constant entreaties as to what the job was about and how I was faring. But I was anxious not to report to her every pang of unhappiness in the employment which she had done so much to promote for me. However, it was not to be all that long before I realised I had had an introduction to a most fulfilling and rewarding occupation in life and that, ultimately, I would have a lot to thank her for.

It happened that suddenly there was a chink of light in the darkness! Around the end of January 1938, Adam said to me: "For reasons which I cannot understand Frank Connett has asked me to check if you would like to work for him, if you do, I must warn you that he will be much stricter with you than I have been."

The person to whom he was referring was a contemporary (certainly not a friend) of Adam. As chief clerk to a set of chambers at Goldsmith Building, Connett had what was almost certainly the most attractive of all senior clerks' jobs – that of managing the most amazing phenomenon the Bar has probably ever seen, Valentine Holmes!

The immediate attraction was that the junior clerk's berth or the 'boy' in that illustrious set of Chambers was an 'in' job at that time. Apart from the reputation of the chambers, Frank Connett was one of the most respected and attractive of all the senior clerks with whom I had by then come into contact. He was extremely personable with a lively wit and sense of humour and commanded attention with his magnetism.

I could not say 'Yes' quickly enough! My desire to work with and for Frank Connett was surpassed only by my need to get away from the Cloisters as soon as possible. I was released to have an interview. Although Goldsmith Building was only twenty yards or so from the Cloisters it represented quite another world so far as I was concerned. Frank Connett greeted me warmly – the discussion took barely a minute.

"The salary is 17/6d (87.5 pence) a week. Don't call me 'Sir' or Mr. Connett', call me Frank, everyone else does. Can you start Monday? If so, I'll have a word with Adam."

CHAPTER TWO

Tom, Dick or Harry

Early in February 1938, I started my new job. On arrival the first thing to be resolved was what I was to be called. Connett said: "What is your name, son?"

"Parsliffe – er, Frank," I ventured.

"No, no, your Christian name?"

"Fran – er, Frank," I said.

"Oh dear it is Frank is it? Well we can't have two Franks around here and I have been here longer than you! We must call you Tom, Dick or Harry. Any preference?"

"No" I said.

"Well then we shall call you Tom."

Hence was born the nickname which has lasted over forty-eight years. Looking back, I should have suggested Bernard my second Christian name, but at that time, it seemed to be a matter of no lasting application. However, in the limited environment of the Temple one comes into contact all the time with contemporaries and the nickname soon catches on. I was not the only one of a number of Juniors or 'Boys' who finished up with names other than their own.

I was immediately in the thick of it all, running across the Strand to the Law Courts, carrying books, briefs and papers under the compelling but pleasant influence of Frank Connett. As in the Cloisters I was the third clerk or boy but there was quite a difference in emphasis. Adam invariably stayed in chambers all day leaving Harold to do the main clerking in the Law Courts, but that was much less than in the Holmes' set.

Here, if required, two people for most of the day in the organisation of the extremely heavy court practice of VH. Frank Connett's number two was a likeable and efficient chap called John Robertshaw. John was the one who stayed put in chambers and was the mechanical sheet-anchor, piloting the endless telephone enquiries, fixing conferences and entering instructions from solicitors. He hardly ever went to court, possibly because he was self-conscious about his harelip which looked (or so John thought) unsightly. He much preferred not being face to face with clients, he was more relaxed and happy dealing with people over the telephone.

It was, therefore, a convenient arrangement for me to be Frank's main assistant at the court end of clerking. I loved running around from one hearing to another and seeing the top advocates of the day in action.

VH had the largest Junior Counsel's practice ever and, as such was constantly engaged with or against these giants. In 1935 he was appointed Junior Counsel to the Treasury, the most coveted job open to the Junior Civil Bar. It required him to act as a standing Junior barrister in all legal civil matters in which the Crown was involved in the King's Bench Division. This included advising and appearing as a crown barrister in court. He was also under the direction of, and required to assist, the Law Officers of the day (the Attorney General and the Solicitor General), with any legal help they might request.

If a case arose of sufficient importance, one or other of the Law Officers would advise with and, perhaps, lead the Treasury Junior in court. But whereas the Law Officers were and are political/legal appointments by the Prime Minister of the day, limited to the life of the Government in power, the Treasury Junior was and is a non-political appointment, held traditionally and normally for no more than seven years. Law Officers are salaried (as with all Cabinet Ministers), but the Treasury junior was, and still is, fee earning; and the term of office was not, and is not, dependent on the Government remaining in power. The fees paid by the Treasury in those days were regulated and derisory. However, the junior could then, but not now, continue with his private practice. Indeed without it, he could hardly survive. VH almost unbelievably, in both 1938 and 1939 reputedly broke all records when his fees totalled £23,000.00 from all sources.

I had the task of typing his quarterly fee sheets to the Treasury! As was the practice of all Government departments, the items on the fee sheet were recorded without the amounts and these were later fixed by the appropriate authorities. The quarterly cheque back from the Treasury was not much more than £500.00 making a total annual income from that source of about £2,000.00. This meant, of course, that his private practice was producing over £20,000.00 a year.

The enormity of this can be judged from the fact that before the War and for a few years after, certain Sunday newspapers were constantly critical of the excessive earnings of leading Silks of the day who could earn as much as £10,000.00 per year.

The ever-important privilege attached to the appointment of Treasury Junior was (and is), that it carries, short of a major disaster, the ultimate reward of an appointment to the High Court Bench. This is usually available after five years of the seven-year contract.

VH was the only incumbent of the office who made it quite clear to the Lord Chancellor when he was offered the job, that he was totally uninterested in being made a High Court Judge. He made it plain that he would only accept on those terms and was, unlike all other Treasury counsel, never made one.

It was believed, at the time, that he wanted to remain a junior member of the Bar throughout his whole legal career but pressure of paperwork finally persuaded him to accept a silk gown in 1945.

Until a year or two ago it was the rule of the profession that whilst a junior could act on his own, a leader had to have a junior in attendance, so that his task in "Silk" was alleviated somewhat in that way. His life at the Bar as a junior was exceptional, almost beyond belief.

On an average, he was in no less than four civil trials a day in cases which were running simultaneously, plus another six or seven summonses or applications. Also he advised (in conference or in writing) an average of another twelve to twenty clients daily.

The specimen diary sheet displayed overleaf is no exaggeration. He had a photographic memory and had no need to read the same papers twice, however long an interval between events.

As far as the court appearances were concerned, he employed, by agreement, all the other members of his chambers as 'devils'. This expression originated some time ago whenever a less busy member of the Bar was asked to assist a more busy one, if the latter was meant to be in two courts at the same time. The devil would be employed as a stand in, sometimes mute but often required to take an active part in the proceedings.

SPECIMEN DIARY SHEET – GOLDSMITH BUILDING, Temple, E.C.4

Wednesday, May 6th, 1939 payable Fee (1939 levels)
V. Holmes Common law matters
9.30 Conference (1 guinea – £1 I shilling)
9.45 (x)
10.00 (x)
10.15 (x)
10.30 Application to Adjourn, (x) 2 guineas (£2 2 shillings)
10.30 (x)
10.30 (x)
10.30 Summons before Judge in Chambers (x) 4 guineas (£4 4 shillings)
10.30 (x)
10.30 (x) cc
10.30 Civil hearing part heard (with x K.C.) (x) 40 guineas (£42)
10.30 (x) cc
10.30 (x) cc
10.30 (With assistance of a member of his Chambers) (x) 35 guineas (£36 15 shillings)
10.30 (x) c
10.30 cc (x) cc
1.30 p.m. Summons before Master (x) 3 guineas (£3 3 shillings)
1.30 (x)
1.30 (x)

1.30 (x)
4.15 Conference (x) 1 guinea (£1 1 shilling)
4.30 (x)
4.45 (x)
5.00 Consultation with Attorney General in Law Courts 2 guineas
(£2 2 shillings)
5.30 Conference (x) 1 guinea (£1 1 shilling)
5.45 (x)

The remainder of the diary sheet would record the professional engagements of all the other members of chambers, usually no more than two items per day.

In his cases VH needed three devils in his average four courts daily. Generally, he would attend all cases instructed as Treasury Junior. In some cases he would use devils as juniors behind leaders, whenever unable to be there himself.

Finally, he would use the devil to take over proceedings when there was no leader and he was held up in another court. Thus, in the latter example, it was possible, say, for VH to open a case for the Plaintiff then run off to another court, leaving his devil to call the appropriate witnesses. He would endeavour to return to cross-examine his opponent's witnesses, or make the final speech to the judge or jury. If not, the devil would have to perform these tasks or, to put it another way, VH would fluctuate his endeavours between all the courts in which he was briefed.

The devils concerned included, for a while:

The Hon Ewen Montague (made a K.C. in 1939 and had a key role in Naval Intelligence during the War). He wrote the fascinating factual story of '*The Man that never Was*' – a compelling tale of perhaps the most successful subterfuge which baffled the Nazis, followed by a more general spy book called '*Top Secret*'. His legal attainments were to be appointed Judge Advocate of the Fleet and Chairman of Hampshire and Middlesex Quarter Sessions.

The Hon T.G. Roche (the son of a law lord) who became a silk. He left the Bar to take up a lucrative legal job in the City.

Mr. Helenus Milmo (later a Q.C. and later still made a High Court Judge).

Mr. Peter Bristow (also destined to be a Silk and High Court Judge) Sir John Senter (later to become a specialist Tax Silk).

VH would attend the court in which his presence was the most vital at any time. For this to be a productive exercise, he needed not only devils to assist in Court but 'tellers' to keep him posted as to the progress of cases in courts in which he was briefed but not actually in attendance. Hence the need for two clerks!

As the supremo Frank Connett was brilliant. He had the knack of assessing, almost without error, after a hushed word with the devil, the timing of the progress of the trial, and the estimation of the moment when VH was needed. He would have me scurrying off at great speed to collect the great man, sometimes when he was on his feet addressing a judge in one court when needed in another. Somehow VH would quickly terminate his submission, without sacrificing the point, make the appropriate bow to the judge, and disappear from the court.

He was the heaviest smoker I have encountered – an average of two packets of fifty Gold Flake cigarettes per day. As he hurried to the next appointed court, he would light up even if the distance between the courts was a matter of only a few feet.

Frank Connett and I developed a form of tic-tac language of signs, along the Law Courts' corridors, which house about twenty courts. Clockwork precision was needed at times to effect his arrival and departure from one court to another. VH was a man of very few words – he often claimed that there really was only one point in most cases and had the strength of legal intellect to 'gamble' (if that be the right word) on one point only. Many times he would produce only one authority recorded in the Law Reports Volume against his opponent's ten or more to prove his case. A sentiment for which I (as his book carrier) was grateful. He had earned the reputation of never misleading judges and seemed to have an uncanny appraisal of exactly what they would wish to hear.

I can recall no judge who showed anything other than the highest respect for VH's integrity and prowess and he was the particular 'pet' of the Lord Chief Justice, Lord Hewitt! His reputation was so great that, almost dangerously, his word would be accepted as 'law' much to the annoyance of his opponents. His knowledge of the law was undoubtedly profound and with his remarkable memory, he was the nearest thing to a human encyclopaedia. In particular, he knew the *'White Book'* (the everyday bible of civil practice and procedure in the High Court) almost completely, often quoting it in court from memory. Again, this was most disarming for his opponents. However, his greatest attribute was considered by many to be his remarkable judgement, based, no doubt, on his extensive knowledge and legal appreciation.

His conferences lasted minutes rather than hours once his (certain) advice had been tendered – he was not a man for small talk. Although very gentle and well-mannered (the judges would never have idolised him, however brilliant, if he had not been), he did not waste time for the sake of public relations. It was unnecessary for him or his clerk to tout for work but he managed to remain on friendly terms with nearly all of his solicitor clients, despite the lack of a 'bedside' manner. Any shortfall there was almost certainly made up by Connett's warm personality.

VH's written opinions were rarely more than about three paragraphs, however long and involved the instructions were. In practice, about two or three sentences would suffice, the advice being simple and to the point. He would avoid the usual style of proving to those instructing him, that he had understood the points raised. This is normally done by repeating verbatim the summary of questions asked, such as 'I am asked to advise whether … etc.' This may take up all of page 1 and perhaps more.

VH would write in his squiggly manuscript something along the lines of:

OPINION

This action will almost certainly succeed. Issue a writ and accept nothing less than £X in settlement. VH

Mostly his few words would be scrawled at the end of the instructions if there was an inch or two of space available. Very rarely would he ask for his paperwork to be typed. On the few occasions when it was necessary, e.g. a draft to go across to the Attorney General, I would have to tap out the material on an ancient Barlock typewriter.

Under Connett's expert tuition, I learned the art of 'watching' cases or checking lists with the emphasis on timing. I also learned how to seek from the judge's clerk or court associate, co-operation in getting the judge to sit early or late or vary his list to assist the tight programme of VH. His reputation and status usually ensured such assistance, but if it was not forthcoming, Connett knew how best to overcome the difficulty with the aid of one of the devils. Frank's good humour and friendly contact with everyone concerned, was the key to this particular success if VH's name was not enough.

Somehow everything worked out – I cannot recall any major disaster occurring during the four years I shared in this remarkable clerking experience. I loved the chance to be involved, however humbly, with the many fashionable cases of the day especially the jury actions for libel, slander, breach of promise etc. VH seemed to be in every one of them going with one or other of the 'big four'. These were old fashioned silks: Sir Patrick Hastings, Mr. Norman Birkett, Sir William Jowett and the one that I rank the most impressive, Sir Stafford Cripps. If one adds to these giants the names of Sir Walter Monkton K.C., Sir Raymond Evershed K.C., (later Master of the Rolls) and Sir Cyril Radcliffe K.C., it will be seen that the leading Bar was then extremely strong.

If time allowed, I would steal a few minutes to go into the courts where these great advocates were performing (whether VH was there or not) and marvel at their different styles of oratory. Sir Patrick was a great showman – he had developed an image over the years with his well-worn wig, and flatly refused to buy a new one, which would have been very white and would have spoilt the aura of experience.

Even in the height of a particularly hot summer when the judges usually invite counsel to remove their wigs, Sir Patrick would very eloquently decline: "Your Lordship's most thoughtful invitation".

Mr. Norman Birkett represented the more sincere and hard-working type of advocate, particularly successful in murder defences. He appeared to be fired by warmth and emotion and a sense of realism appealing to the jury's human feelings.

Sir William Jowett, an ugly man, looked classically strong and forbidding. Tall and upright, he lacked warmth and emotion, unlike Birkett, and relied on a powerfully and coldly delivered argument with a strong clear voice to prove his points. He was not very popular.

Sir Stafford Cripps, also tall and upright, was the great intellect and the most political. Like Gerald Gardiner later, but probably even better, he portrayed the confident self-assured master of English and belief in his cause. Arguably the best lawyer of the mentioned giants, he was a great loss to the Bar when he moved on to other pastures.

Sir William Monckton, by far the most friendly of the lot, was a very stylish commercial type leader, not always to the forefront of publicity in the courts, being involved with Arbitration and Enquiries and suchlike.

Sir Cyril Radcliffe and Sir Raymond Evershed, who concentrated on the more specialised Chancery Division work, were not household names like the others but were, nevertheless, at the very top of their professional life in Lincoln's Inn.

All had one thing in common – they had an unwavering regard for VH. Not once, as I recall, did any one of them complain when VH deposited a devil behind them in court. What each wanted, above all else, was the advice and guidance which VH would give, outside court hours if necessary, as to the merits of the case in law and the tactical approach required in Court

I remember Sir Stafford Cripps calling at Goldsmith Buildings one evening at about 5 o'clock and asking Frank Connett whether, on the assumption that VH was not necessarily going to attend as his junior next day as instructed, he could have a few words with him overnight. Frank immediately and rightly offered to get VH to call on Sir Stafford in his chambers (as is the etiquette with silks and juniors), but Sir Stafford was quite happy to waive the appropriate recognised practice. He was soon in with VH and after only a few minutes came out content with the advice he had received. I got the impression that Sir Stafford was VH's favourite leader. They certainly got on well together and constituted a most formidable team, especially if the case was very involved.

VH was a man of unimpressive appearance. He was not very tall and looked rather shoddy, with balding hair and an ugly nose. No one looked less likely to be a successful barrister.

On one occasion when a new solicitor from the Home Counties instructed him to attend on a 1.30 p.m. Summons, Frank had to say over the telephone that, just for once, VH could not personally attend and it would have to be covered by a devil. Usually VH would not need devils for the Summonses, because he was adept at dealing with them in about two minutes flat (assisted by his White Book knowledge, which the Masters would accept as gospel). The Summonses were listed at 1.30 p.m. in another part of the Law Courts, not far from the King's Bench corridors, so they did not interfere with trials which recommenced after the lunch time adjournment, at 2.00 p.m.

But on this particular day VH was running an appeal in the House of Lords at Westminster – too far away to take in the Law Courts' Summonses – hence the need for a devil. However at the last moment, and with no time to give the good news to the solicitor, VH found after all, that having finished early at Westminster, he could get back in time. He duly arrived and relieving his colleague of the papers, went into the Master's Room, dealt with the matter in the usual brief way, and proceeded to his next summons in another room.

Later that day, the solicitor rang Frank to say that while he had not objected to the use of a devil, in the circumstances as explained, and although the summons was successful, he thought it his duty to object to the use of a 'very unkempt and withdrawn old man who didn't say much and mumbled his way through the proceedings'.

Even when VH was addressing the court, he had a habit of letting his gown drape off the shoulder on one side and made no attempt to look elegant. At a cursory glance, the casual onlooker would not spare him a second thought. It was only after listening to him perform and to realise that his words were being absorbed fully and appreciatively by judge or jury that the magnitude of the man became apparent. His oratory was sheer sanity, simple but totally effective, with the minimum of words.

After the last conference had finished each evening, Frank Connett would go into VH's room with a huge armful of briefs and papers which John had accepted and entered up during the day. With VH standing with his back to the fireplace and the inevitable cigarette between his lips, Frank would read out quickly the name of the cases, old or new, which required VH's attention.

The briefs for the next day's court cases and the papers for the conferences would be placed in two large holdall zip bags ready to be taken to VH's home. This was my last task every night. VH's flat was about two hundred yards away on the third floor of No. 3 Temple Gardens. He had converted it into luxury accommodation overlooking the river across the Embankment. Mrs. Holmes would greet me with a cheery: "good evening," as I deposited the work in the hall. I would then go off to Temple Station and home. The bags would be collected by me next morning at about 8.45 a.m. and returned to Chambers. There, John Robertshaw, would empty one on his desk while I looked after the other. An average of about 15 sets of papers would have been done overnight by the great man. These would consist of Advices, Opinions, draft pleadings and notes for leaders. John and I would then spend the next fifteen minutes or so telephoning the solicitors concerned to inform them that their papers were ready for collection.

His reputation for a twenty-four-hour service became legend, and was balm for certain solicitors who may have allowed themselves to get a little late with the instructions for Counsel's advice for which their lay clients were pressing.

At about 6 o'clock, after I had left with the bag, VH and Frank Connett would walk together to El Vino's (the Pomeroys of Mortimer's 'Rumpole' series) for a well-earned drink. They were the closest of friends. Never have a barrister and clerk been so wedded.

Many years later Frank confided that if he could have his time over again, he would not have allowed himself to get into such a compulsive association. This was not meant as a criticism of VH so much as a warning against falling into a daily habit which could become, as in his case, too demanding and taxing! But during the period of my employment there (1938 to 1942) and a for a few years thereafter they spent every weekday and evening together as well as most Saturdays and occasional Sundays.

The routine, at least up until the start of the War, was that on most mid-week evenings, after a couple of sherries (VH) and ports (Frank), a minicab driver, on a full retainer by VH, would park his car, which was then possible, right outside El Vino's. There it would be left for about fifteen minutes whilst the driver, Bob, had a drink with his fare at the back of the wine bar. The three of them, together with any other invited friends, would leave by car for an evening at the 'dogs'.

I remember that the tracks frequented were all coincidentally, those with 'W' as their first letter. These were Wembley, Wimbledon, White City, West Ham, Walthamstow and their 'home track' Wandsworth.

After the War, when the routine was revived and though I had moved on to another job, I was privileged on about six occasions to be one of the friends or guests at these 'dog' parties. We would leave El Vino's at about 6.45pm and arrive at Wandsworth soon after 7 o'clock. There we would be shown up to VH's private box overlooking the winning post. It wasn't as lavish as a theatre box, but was most comfortable with four or five wicker chairs, with VH claiming the one which was right next to an aperture into the adjoining bar. This meant that all he had to do to order drinks was to stand up. His face would then be on the appropriate level to summon the barmaid through the hole. His tips were so generous that his appearance was enough for immediate service. He insisted on paying for every round but also demanded that, having chosen one's first drink, one should not change throughout the evening. I never did understand why that should be so, but it was one of his quirks. Hot food would be produced on trays, usually fish and chips.

I clearly remember the usual pattern: I would invest two shillings (10 pence) on the Tote, Frank would do £1.00 or a ten shilling forecast and VH would have a reversed forecast of at least £5.00 each way. Most times he would ask Frank or me to put on the bet for him or collect any returns. He sometimes lost over £100 but when his luck was in, his winnings could be as much as £300 or more (The equivalent profit would now, I guess, be in the region of a few thousand pounds). After each race, Frank would invite VH to work out in his head the forecast dividend from the mass of figures displayed on the Tote board at one end of the track before it was officially announced. Mentally VH would deduct from the total, the expenses' percentage and tax and divide the reduced total by the number of winning units. He, invariably, beat the declared dividend by a full minute and was accurate in nine cases out of ten.

After the races, Bob drove everyone back to the Temple, stopping if time allowed at a pub in Westminster for a night cap. I was dropped off at Temple station, then VH at the foot of his building and Frank kept Bob on to go all the way to Pinner where he (and Bob) lived.

It was at this point, in the early days, that having been out all evening, VH would tackle one of the two bags until about 2.00 a.m. (assisted by black coffee and a meagre sandwich). He needed very little sleep and by about 5.00 a.m. he would rise and, again with black coffee, would grapple with the other bag.

Long before I arrived to collect the work he would have had a sparse breakfast (probably one piece of toast and the inevitable black coffee) before leaving for chambers. His daily lunch would consist of a half glass of Guinness and half a chicken sandwich purchased from El-Vino's. Noticeably, he would bite out only the soft bread and chicken, leaving the crust untouched, rather like a child.

121

I cannot recall the dogs' trips being scrubbed because of pressure of work. On the rare occasions they did not go, it was because the weather was bad or that VH was tired, never that he needed the time to do the required homework.

On most Saturdays, after working in the morning and a brief pub lunch in Fleet Street, both VH and Frank would go off to horse racing at the nearest racecourse to London, finishing up at the dogs in the evening.

On some Sundays VH would go out to Pinner to join Frank for a local lunchtime drink in the 'Headstone Hotel', followed by lunch at his house before coming back to town and yet more work in the late afternoon or early evening.

He was clearly a lonely man, although married with two children. Frank Connett was also married with children. Neither spent much time with their families, but deriving much pleasure in each other's company and with some of their legal friends around the Temple. These were mainly other clerks, rather than barristers, VH being somewhat reluctant to mingle socially with his legal peers or contemporaries – or perhaps it was just shyness!

Our clerks room was typical of the time – not much room and no effective planning with papers and ledgers strewn over the desks and floors, despite John's attempts to keep the place tidy. Flanagan and Allen arrived one evening to consult VH with some legal point and Bud Flanagan, seeing the mess all over the floor said to his partner: "Ches, let's sue these buggers – they've pinched our filing system".

Despite the pressure of work, Frank would invite me to stand most evenings in the doorway of our room and act as goalkeeper to his centre-forward skills. He would screw up the paper bag which had contained our tea buns from the local Lyons Tea Shop into a tight ball. It was very resilient and just right to be kicked at great speed from his side of the room. Frank had been a fine footballer in his youth and I found myself almost pelted nonstop by his barrage. I managed to save a few, but those which eluded me (the goals) would bounce against VH's door before I could retrieve 'the ball' and feed it back to Frank. This would occur no matter who was in VH s room in conference. His clients must have wondered what extraneous activities our chambers were noted for.

VH never once complained although Helenus Milmo, who occupied a side room, occasionally came out to enquire what was the latest score.

The social climate engendered by VH and Frank Connett in chambers was remarkable – the key note being hard work and a bit of a laugh with no traumas. Only once, when I was a minute or two late delivering his robes to him, did VH scald me rather severely. Later he apologised, but the message had gone home. His programme did not allow for any delay, however short.

I had not been there long when a sweepstake was organised on the Derby. Everyone was asked to subscribe five shillings for a ticket. Being the Boy I was the only exception – they gave me a free go. My horse 'Boise Roussel' romped home and I was the recipient of about £4. It was decided in future that everyone should pay for their ticket, Boy or not!

Such was life in Goldsmith Building in 1938 and up to September 1939. Alas, it suddenly came to an end with the outbreak of War, or at least it drastically changed. Overnight VH lost his team of colleagues, the devils. All of them, I think, were in some reserve or other and had to report to their units. John Robertshaw was immediately conscripted, being just the appropriate age. Life was never quite the same again. But, as will be seen, VH and Frank (and Tom) battled on undaunted.

CHAPTER THREE
The balloon goes up!

Everything seemed to happen so fast. Domestically, we now had to put into effect that which we had been taught, but with typical British optimism, thought would never be required. At least the die was cast! The War with Germany was a fact and we had to adjust ourselves to it.

With resignation, but not mournfully, we checked our air-raid shelters, ration books and gas masks; tightened up our black-out and obeyed the authorities with a number of orders and instructions to put us on a war footing.

Sadly this included the immediate evacuation of children away from London. My three younger sisters, Eileen, Theresa and Angela (aged 13, 10 and 5 years respectively) went off to Egham in Surrey. My poor mother, always a cheerful person, put on a very brave face as she waved them goodbye with their nametags around their necks. My older brother, Jack, was called up after a few weeks and joined the Royal Engineers, leaving me the only one of five children at home with my parents.

My father had a few months earlier, reached the magic figure of twenty-five years' service as a policeman and had elected to serve, as was then the option, another year before taking his retirement. He was told that that was not now possible, health permitting, he would continue his duties for the duration of the War. He did not seem to mind. It was all so unreal. Even on that Sunday morning at about 11 o'clock, when Neville Chamberlain broadcast the dramatic news that we were now at War, very few people recognised it as the start of a five-year involvement. Either we would blow the German war effort to blazes or in some other way Hitler would see the error of his ways and capitulate. It would not be long before we could resume our normal way of life. Everywhere there was an air of excitement with not a semblance of fear of defeat.

Although Chamberlain had been proved wrong with his 'Peace in our Time' statement at Heston airport on his return from negotiations with Hitler the previous year, there was a confident mood around that we could and would show him what the British bulldog does when finally aroused

Overnight the calm English reserve was cast aside in the common goal to get on and repeat what we had done to Germany during the Great War. We gave up some of our iron and steel, such as pots and pans, as well as our railings to be smelted down and made into guns and other tools of war. We became, all at once, non-political and intensely patriotic. Strangers on trains began to talk to each other and a general air of camaraderie and 'togetherness' pervaded all around.

In the back gardens of homes such as ours in Fairfoot Road, Bow, after the War had been announced, almost everyone had gathered to discuss the traumatic news, over the fences:

"They must be mad to take us on again!"

"The RAF is probably bombing the Germans right now!"

"It'll be all over in a few weeks, you'll see – Britain and France will be too much for them".

They were the kind of remarks which echoed from neighbour to neighbour.

Suddenly at about 11.30 a.m. the air-raid siren sounded. No one could believe it! After what seemed an age of shocked silence, there gradually emerged an ever-growing upswell of incredulous comments:

"Christ! The bastards!"

"What a bloody nerve."

"How dare they?!"

But slowly it dawned on everyone that, just possibly, enemy planes might appear overhead at any moment.

Some, like my father, acted with great calm, urging that no-one panicked. The more he beseeched them, the more one or two, and especially my mother, disobeyed. With uncontrolled emotions and a wild shriek she disappeared down into the Anderson shelter at the end of the garden, like a bat out of hell.

My old Grandmother, who lived with us, was a tough old bird, but not to be outdone by her daughter, also shrieked and pushed her way into the shelter. She reappeared a few seconds later and announced to my father that, as we could be marooned under siege for perhaps days, she must get some essentials from the house. Rushing up to her room she emerged, after a minute or two, with a bottle of Black and White whisky wrapped in a blanket.

"What the hell have you got there?" enquired my father.

"Medicinal supplies," answered Gran.

She ran along the garden path back to the Anderson, having no regard for her mature age or for her back which she always claimed gave her so much pain. Suddenly the bottle slipped out of the blanket and smashed to smithereens on the path.

"You stupid woman," said my father, not averse himself to an occasional tot of Scotch. There followed more expletives, too severe to repeat here. After just a few more minutes the 'All Clear' sounded. Relieved faces appeared out of the shelters and joined the 'brave ones' who had defied the warning by remaining in the open. The crescendo of comments was renewed, after a few seconds as the obvious relief sunk in:

"There, what did I say?"

"They've turned turtle and gone back"

"No, more likely the RAF have bashed them out of the skies!"

"That'll teach 'em."

"Let's get to the radio to find out how many we've shot down!"

In fact no German planes came anywhere near and clearly it was a false alarm. Little did we know then how unprepared we really were. Some months later when the bombing of London (and the East End in particular) started, there was hardly an anti-aircraft gun heard for some days or even weeks, and the indiscriminate destruction took place mainly unchecked.

Meanwhile the phoney war had started. It meant that whilst we expected the worst, nothing much appeared to have happened as a direct threat to us. Slowly the Nazis went about the business of annexing our European allies one by one, before turning their attention to Britain. Nevertheless our lives changed, in some ways, almost at once.

As the darker evenings of autumn were upon us, soon to be followed by winter, the black-out became more restrictive. Our social life in Bow, never very much, was reduced to small functions like 'hops' and whist drives in the church hall, behind darkened windows. On moonless nights it was an eerie experience to grope one's way home, with car headlights being nothing more than down-turned slits.

My father and I developed the habit of having card sessions at home – notably Solo and Brag. These included one of my local friends and the curate from the Catholic Church in Bow Road, who loved to come over and have a gamble – much to my father's astonishment! We made the best of it, but as so many friends of mine were joining up, the heart was torn out of our teenage lifestyle, such as it was.

In the Temple, similar changes were taking place. The air-raid shelters were different from those in our homes. I don't recall any Andersons in the offices of the City. Mainly the basements of buildings were converted for the purpose, with literally hundreds of sandbags stacked up outside.

One of our below ground rooms, previously occupied by pupils, became the shelter and later when fire-watching began, it was our bedroom as and when sleep was possible. We received a never-ending stream of orders and directions from the Inner Temple, our landlords, concerning everything necessary for our welfare, safety, and hopefully the continuation of our business.

The first absolute essential was the black out. It immediately became a very serious offence if a chink of light, however small, was detected by the police. It wasn't long before fashionable London stores were being prosecuted for lighting offences at Bow Street and other London Magistrates Courts.

Valentine Holmes became in great demand to represent some of these big concerns and plead in mitigation. This was one of the forms of barrister representation which appeared to me to be misjudged. Suppose that a Bond Street jeweller's night watchman had left a window slightly open and it showed a sliver of light. The shop would be prosecuted and they would probably instruct high-class solicitors from the West End or the City, who in turn would choose someone like VH to attend court.

The Magistrate, knowing of VH's standing and reputation, would almost certainly take the view that if they could afford VH's fees, they could cough up a steep fine! This would result in an order for a payment of probably thousands instead of hundreds of pounds. It would have been far better to send a young pupil to say: "Sorry – it will not happen again," and go down for a much smaller fine.

Our chambers were stripped almost overnight of practically everyone apart from the 'Boss' and a few pupils. Most other sets became bereft of a large part of their numerical strength; in some cases so severely that amalgamations had to take place, perhaps three or four juniors would be left without a clerk, or a clerk with only one or two barristers. Over a comparatively short period of time I would guess about one third of the practising Bar had joined up, the fraction increasing sharply as the war progressed.

The General Council of the Bar, the governing body, were concerned that the barristers who had left to serve their country (either by volunteering or subscription) would lose out to those who were still practising and issued a directive to all sets of chambers in an effort to compensate.

Their suggestion (I do not think it was as strong as an order) was that solicitors should be encouraged to continue to send instructions and briefs to chambers in the name of the barrister of their choice, whether he was still there or in the services. If he was away, and with their consent, a non-serving colleague would be invited to do the job of work, sharing the fees when paid with the absent one. It was intended that the gesture should not be limited to within the chambers and that generally, across the Bar, it should be recognised as an established etiquette.

At first it worked very well, everyone adopting the right spirit and helping their serving brothers with a build-up of a reserve of cash as well as helping to retain the all-important goodwill. A great deal revolved around the clerk, who had to keep a sharp look out to pilot the scheme fairly by persuading the solicitors accordingly and to control the flow of fees. It was indeed very reassuring and pleasing to barristers in the services to receive a letter from the clerk stating that some amount of money had been paid into their bank account through the good offices of colleagues around the Temple.

But, regrettably, this most creditable practice gradually disintegrated after a year or so; human nature being what it is! What usually happened was that the solicitor got used to the substitute barrister and began sending him papers in his own name. It was not permissible for the clerk to interfere with this turn of events without the consent of all concerned. In many cases it was the solicitor who insisted on leaving it alone, because he wanted to 'reward' the new man for doing a fine job assisting in earlier matters.

Then, of course, the clerks were being called up and consequently the continuity might be lost or weakened; the Chambers' junior or substitute (perhaps following an amalgamation) would not have the 'feel' of the position as strongly as the established clerk. Some did better than others, especially if they were too old to serve.

One clerk managed to keep the good work going for most of the War. He was unfit to serve in the forces and found himself by Christmas, 1939, with just one barrister and a pupil or two only. His name was Fred Ponsford, senior clerk at that time to Mr. Cartwright-Sharpe and close friend of Frank Connett. He had a great deal of charm and a persuasive tongue. He managed to retain all, or nearly all, of his chambers' solicitors' patronage by following the Bar Council's suggestion. He got them to send their instructions to his chambers with the names of all his serving Junior barristers. Then he worked tirelessly going from one set of chambers to another, getting the odd barrister, through his clerk, to take the odd brief on the 50% basis. He called on us nearly every day and produced briefs for our pupils (some marked at only two guineas), coming back later to collect the papers when the cases were finished, in order to return them to the solicitors, collect the fees and make the apportionment.

With this tight control and in this way he kept the names of his various principals to the forefront of the minds of his chambers' clients. The fact that the returning warriors found their chambers on such a solid bedrock was due, in no small measure, to Fred's ardent endeavours.

The chambers opposite ours on the ground floor of Goldsmith Building was reduced to just one person, Mr. Arthur Beecroft, a barrister of about 45 years of age. He immediately applied for, and was granted, admission to VH's chambers 'for the duration' (as we used to refer to the War). He took over the room previously occupied by Ewen Montagu. One or two young people were also 'in' which gave us at least the nucleus of a team. But, with respect to those concerned, they did not constitute the powerhouse of the earlier devils – all of whom, without exception, carved themselves colourful practices as a result of the experience gained assisting VH, as well as their own undoubted ability.

With his limited chambers assistance and the enormous pressure of the Treasury job now that we were at War, VH reached saturation point. The two Law Officers (the Attorney General – Sir Donald Somerville K.C., and the Solicitor General – Sir Terence O'Connor K.C.) had to answer to Parliament with the introduction of endless new legislation, notably the Defence Regulations, covering a wide spectrum of emergency powers which the Government, perforce, had to take on. This included such things as 'aliens' and 'internment'.

Advice was sought urgently on the drafting and implementation of these regulations. They leaned very heavily on VH. At first, he seemed to be in an endless series of consultations, with one or other or both of them together with senior Treasury officials.

Furthermore, as the standing junior barrister representing the Crown, it was he who had to deal with every case where individuals sued the War Office, the Admiralty or the Air Ministry for personal injuries sustained when knocked down by service lorries.

With the ever-increasing number of vehicles being deployed for the War effort, unfortunately but inevitably more and more people suffered in this way. If a writ was issued against the Government for compensation, whatever the cause or complaint, VH had the task of settling the formal written defence and, if necessary, to represent the Treasury in court. In practice, very few reached a trial; VH's advice on offers of settlement, which accompanied his draft defences, would be acted upon and almost invariably produced an acceptable settlement.

For this extra burden of papers he had no additional assistance at that time from his fellow barristers. With many successful juniors joining up, VH was in yet greater demand in the private sector of his practice, even if it included the ill-conceived briefing in 'lighting' summonses. These short hearings had to be fixed, with help from the appropriate court listing officers, either before the High Court sat or during the lunchtime adjournment, similar to the 1.30 p.m. summonses already referred to.

The volume of his civil work increased, both as regards court cases and (written and oral) advice. Looking back, after some 45-years or so, I find it extremely difficult to recall exactly how he managed to get through it all. VH was never ill and there was absolutely no sign or evidence that any client suffered in the slightest degree because of being only one of dozens daily seeking the best legal assistance from him.

As the Treasury work remorselessly grew during 1940, 1941 and 1942, VH was allowed to release a little of it to one Mr. J.P. Ashworth, a junior barrister with chambers just around the corner in Hare Court. He had the approval of the appropriate authorities to come to the aid of VH and when, in 1945, the latter gave up the Treasury job, J.P. Ashworth was duly appointed in his place.

After the War when Mr. Roger Wynn (brother of Godfrey Wynn, the author) followed J.P. Ashworth as the Treasury Junior, the level of Government legal work was such that it was no longer possible to double up with a private practice – at least Roger Wynn thought so, and duly gave it up! His successors followed his lead. In fact, it is now officially prohibited, although it is doubtful whether the volume could have been much heavier than during the War.

Also the more recent ones have had the advantage of assistance from a panel of six other junior barristers chosen on merit (although such helpers can and do continue with their private work). When one considers that all the Treasury Juniors since VH (some eight or so in number) were of the calibre who later became, in turn, noted High Court Judges and yet found it necessary to have such help, it makes VH's War time endeavours even more remarkable.

CHAPTER FOUR
Clerks room capers

John's departure from the scene presented us with an immediate problem. However, after a short deliberation Frank promoted me to the second clerk's berth, four or five years before one would normally expect it; but times were not normal and the early challenge was there to be grasped.

It would have been almost impossible, anyway, to find 23 or 24-year-old replacements because of conscription, and the issue was further aggravated by the decision not to have a number three clerk. So I had to do both jobs. It is true that the overall number of barristers was drastically reduced, but VH was almost a set of chambers on his own and the pressure on the clerks room was noticeably increased.

It meant, of course, that Frank and I could not be in the Law Courts together any more, one of us had to man the shop. We shared the various duties. Judges and court officials, who had been helpful in the past, were now even more so, not only with VH but with us as well. They appreciated that the Bar was under severe strain because of the War and their tolerance was necessary for the survival of our legal system.

As with the attitude in the East End, there was in the Temple no marked depression and the same cheerfulness was apparent all around. Churchill's name was being mentioned more and more, not as a 'warmonger' (so wrongly inferred by some people in the past), but as a vital link in our deliverance, especially when he was appointed First Lord of the Admiralty by Chamberlain. Somehow we knew that he was to play an ever-increasing role in our affairs.

No one exuded more optimism as to the outcome of the War, and self-assured confidence in all fields of adjustment than Frank Connett.

Everything was taken in his stride with minimum effort. He maintained his sense of humour and fun. This was more apparent when he was basic rather than subtle and if some of his jokes got a good laugh, he would repeat them many times before finally rejecting them. I have often been accused of over-telling a good story – I must assume that I caught the habit from my hero, Connett.

He was also a great practical joker. His normal pattern was to subject any newcomers (and this included Arthur Beecroft) to a series of over-powering leg-pulls or embarrassing moments. Frank would start with the mundane 'telephone directory' ploy. He would leave the door of the clerks room about five or six inches ajar and place the thick book across the top of the of the door and resting on the frame. This was on the assumption that the next one to enter was the chosen victim. As the victim pushed open the door, the book would drop solidly on to his head, accompanied by uncontrollable laughter from the clerks room. The deed would be repeated again and again over a few days until, finally, the poor chap would learn to catch the book or wear a very large plaster on his forehead, forcing Frank to desist. Sometimes the wrong person would come in! It was quite an education to listen to Frank explain, in all seriousness, to a respected client who was rubbing his head, how it was that one of our volumes of the Post Office directories had inadvertently been left on top of the door.

When flustered, he had a very slight stutter which enhanced the performance. The next attack would be in the form of 'mock instructions' from a solicitor to the proposed victim. We would type a backsheet brief with made up names and details but looking as authentic as possible. It would state the time and the name of the court that the barrister was required to attend (usually very early next morning in a distant place like Carlisle or Penzance). The names of the parties would be fictitious and the papers to go with the backsheet would be very scant and utterly misleading; just a few odd letters and documents from any old legal papers lying around in the clerks' room. The limited brief would state: 'that shortness of time has not allowed your instructing solicitors to prepare a proper outline of the case, except to say that it is an action for forfeiture, (or some other complicated point of law) and 'would Counsel please get to court early and consult the lay client for further information and then represent him accordingly.' The name of the barrister would be displayed on the sheet with an absurdly small fee, such as, 'five guineas to include expenses'. At the foot of the backsheet, as is customary, would be typed the name of the solicitors. We would choose a high-powered firm who (as the victim would know), could, if impressed, 'make him'. Care was taken to ensure that the last reasonable train had already left London at the time then the Brief was presented to the unsuspecting junior with the encouraging words: "You're lucky! This could be the breakthrough for you."

"But how do I get there?" would be the reasonable reply.

"I don't know – if there are no convenient trains get a pal to run you there tonight by car or motorbike, but do get there somehow – it's your big chance," was the unhelpful retort.

Frantic telephone calls to home for pyjamas and toothbrush etc., and to fiancée or girlfriend to cancel the evening's social engagement would follow a desperate attempt to learn something about 'forfeiture' from text books in chambers before confronting the travel problem. Only as the unfortunate barrister, in a state of near collapse, was about to leave chambers would Frank Connett, with a great grin, let on that it was all a joke!

Even if the barrister was suspicious of the validity of the instructions, he was most unlikely to challenge this kind of briefing, because often it was very real. It did happen, from time to time, that respectable solicitors found themselves in need of barristers to go a long way at short notice and if the budget was limited, the fee offered would be non-profitable. It was so difficult for young Counsel to get started in those days that the introduction to a firm of solicitors far outweighed any monetary gain.

The leg-pull was, of course, rather cruel but in fairness to Frank it must be mentioned that his considerable influence with good solicitors produced many legitimate and rewarding instructions for a number of young members of chambers and pupils who, thereby, were given their chance!

Arthur Beecroft was not the type of barrister to became one of VH's devils. Although quite pleased to be the recipient of the odd job of work falling from the great man's table he was too old or disinclined to get involved with the pressure of the 'rat race' and settled mainly for a quiet life. Who could blame him? Not very tall, he had a military bearing, and was very squat and tough. In his younger days he had been a solid rugby player. We found him a loveable character, but because he was slightly eccentric, he became an obvious butt for Connett's pranks.

Beecroft used to augment his modest Bar earnings by acting as a poor man's legal adviser to the *News of the World*. For this service he was paid a few hundred pounds a year. Every week the Sunday newspaper would send round to chambers, in Arthur Beecroft's name, a batch of letters from their readers with everyday problems and seeking advice on legal remedies. His comments were limited to two or three lines only and the questions and answers would be printed as a kind of agony column in the next issue of the paper. Some were too stupid for words. For example:

Worried from Tunbridge Wells writes:
"My wife has just become pregnant, although we have not had sexual intercourse for eighteen months. Am I right in assuming that she has been unfaithful to me?"

Or Agitated from Cheam asks:
"My neighbour has thrown his dead cat over the fence into my garden. What action do you advise I take?" (Beecroft's answer would be something like throw it back.)

The job itself was not very taxing to his legal talents, because if the problem was an awkward one, all he had to do as a reply was to say: "See a solicitor".

Periodically he would come into the clerks room to say that he rarely got any interesting letters to answer from the paper's readers, most of them being very dull. Frank decided that we should remedy the situation, especially as Beecroft was getting just a little tired of the 'phone directory' treatment (I don't think it even hurt him that much) so we 'manufactured' an appropriate letter which would give him food for thought.

One day, when he was out at lunch, we slipped it into the middle of the bundle which had arrived that morning from the *News of the World*, and was on his desk. Our letter, written in nondescript handwriting, went something like this:

"29 Peabody Buildings,
Shadwell, S.E.
April 7th, 1940.

Dear *'News of the World'*

Can you please help me with a problem? While digging deep over at my allotment the other day, my spade struck a large object which was covered with grime and has obviously been there for a long time. When I got home and washed it, I saw that it was made of earthenware and had, on its side, some kind of inscription, which I think is of ancient origin. I have been studying it tor some days – it looks like: Ill SAPI SSPO TAN DABI GONE GO. Can you tell me whether you think it is a valued Roman urn and having found it, am I the rightful legal owner and what do you think the letters mean? I cannot work it out!

Yours,

Fred Smith."

It was not long before Arthur Beecroft came out to us with the comment: "Chaps! What about this one? It is not the usual type. Can you help?" We displayed only a mild interest in it. For quite a while, and holding up the return of the bundle to the newspaper, he could be seen avidly studying the inscription in the hope of breaking the code. Finally, just as he was giving up rescue was at hand.

"I've got it," said Frank. "If you move the letters slightly it reads: 'It is a piss pot and a big one too.'"

"You're right," said Beecroft gleefully and hastened back to his room to complete his answers. We noticed that the *News of the World* did not print it the following Sunday, much to Beecroft's surprise

He would supply his answers with the assistance of an old portable typewriter, which he used with just two fingers.

On one occasion, sometime later, when Beecroft had been rather persistent in pressing for something unreasonable, Frank decided to take further action. He put a speck of Gloy, the office glue, on each of the keys of the typewriter, while Beecroft was out of the room. He returned eventually, announcing that he would like to be left undisturbed to get on with his 'Newses' as he called them. After a second or two he rushed from his room, screaming with rage at the audacity of his clerks to interfere with his work in this way. He went below to the closet to wash the muck from his hands. As soon as he had gone, Frank painted more glue on to his door handle and covered it with some soot from the open fireplace. Beecroft returned and, imploring us to leave him in peace, grabbed the handle! When he realised what had now happened, he rushed into the clerks room and propelled himself through the air like a missile, directing his body at me (no doubt thinking that I was the main culprit). Although I was much taller than he, his bulk was like a lump of granite. He got me pinned against the wall, winding me in the process. It wasn't long before he had me face down on the ground with him straddled over me in a kind of 'Boston Crab' wrestling hold. I thought my back would break. When he finally released me, by now a heap of bruised flesh and bones, he rose and announced that: "On reflection I am not sure that it was Tom who did the foul deed." By this time Frank had vacated the clerks room in some haste. It was some time before we gathered the courage to tease him further.

CHAPTER FIVE

I become a minder

The black-out, of course, had put an end to the visits to the 'Dogs' – at least in the evenings, but VH and Frank continued to frequent horse racing and dogs on Saturday afternoons in daylight.

However, neither was a great diner except for an occasional trip to the old Oddeninos restaurant in the West End; nor were they keen theatre goers, so they confined their social activities mainly to around the Temple area. They liked the atmosphere of the local hostelries but never did I see them the worse for drink. They would play out time in El Vinos (8.00 p.m. closing) and adopt the habit of then moving to one or two pubs slightly sheltered from cosmopolitan Fleet Street.

It had been considered by some, although there has been no firm directive from above, to be *infra dig* for barristers to be seen imbibing in one or two of the nearby houses, but El Vinos was not regarded as 'out of bounds' except to the higher level of judges.

VH, not one to be a blind disciple of snobbery, nevertheless felt that a more discreet venue was more to his liking. One of these was the 'Essex Head' (now the 'Edgar Wallace') just off the Strand, by St. Clement Dane's church. But the favourite was the Mitre – a few yards up Chancery Lane (now sadly no more – I think it became and still is an Italian restaurant). The latter had a pin table, which was for VH the nearest substitute, albeit a poor one, for the Dogs. It was, in any event, a release from the strain of the day's toil for him to relax and play the machine. He would compete with his barrister clerk friends and others in scoring the highest total of points. The usual stake was 3d (old money) – but woe betide anyone who, having accepted the challenge, 'forgot to part with the 3d if VH won. He was always generous in paying for most of the rounds of drinks, but he could not abide a 'welcher', even if he did not give the loser much time to change a half-a-crown to discharge his debt.

Thus the new pattern for the social side of the VH/Frank partnership took shape during 1940. As I was then a bit older I was occasionally invited to join them and such evenings were very enjoyable.

Soon the Inns of Court, as with the rest of the City, invited volunteers to stay up one night a week and mind their buildings from fire bombs. Frank's many friends, including Fred Ponsford, quickly offered their services and chose Friday night as the best evening and the Essex Head as the best venue (when not putting out incendiaries) to develop their darts skills. Quite a club of clerks was formed. Frank Connett was very popular with this particular batch of colleagues and they constantly pressed him to join them with these 'sacrifices'. Perhaps because he felt 'wedded' to VH on weekday evenings he reluctantly declined, but when the bombing of London started in the autumn of 1940 fire watching became compulsory.

He invited me to go with him to the Inner Temple to register, hoping for both of us to get in on the 'Essex Head' bandwagon. Alas, it was too late – Friday was more popular with most people than we had thought. In fact the only nights left were Saturday and Sunday. VH, despite his crushing Government work, also had to register and decided that Sunday was probably the best night for him. As Frank pointed out, it meant that he could work more quietly in his usual chambers room all evening (unless required to fight fires) and sleep downstairs in the air-raid shelter, where we had installed two single beds. Frank and I plumped for Saturday, which we thought would be a bit more lively than Sunday, and we were duly registered.

We would work through the morning until about 1 o'clock when I would go home to Bow (no more than half an hour's journey) returning at 6 p.m. to report for duty. Frank would go off and join VH for the afternoon, finishing up with me for our night vigil.

One of my morning tasks was to collect, in an old barrister's robe bag, twelve-quart bottles of Watney's Light Ale from Peele's pub (which also no longer exists) situated then on the corner of Fetter Lane. The bottles would be placed in our basement shelter, just below the window ledge to protect them from blast. They augmented the cocktail cupboard which VH had set up in the room for all our benefit over the weekend.

When signing on each week we were greeted by our Chief Fire Warden, a cheerful Welshman named Gwillam, who was also the Head Porter of the Inner Temple. We were under his supervision throughout. He would give us a blanket and four shillings and sixpence, which amount was meant to defray the cost of keeping body and soul together overnight. He was a friendly chap who knew us well – indeed Frank thought it prudent to keep on good terms with him, so we would present him with one of our bottles of beer to fortify himself during the night.

After depositing our blankets in chambers, if things were quiet, we would repair to the 'Cock Tavern', just around the corner. There we would be joined for the evening by some of Frank's friends. He suggested that I should buy the first round of drinks with my allowance, after which he would foot the bill, for all later expenses, whatever they may be. We looked forward very much to such evenings, especially when (as the bombing had not yet reached its zenith) we became a little more adventurous with our fire watching enjoyment, if that is not a contradiction in terms.

The 'Stoll' about five minutes' walk away in Kingsway, was a leading Music Hall in London at that time, but was not overpacked on Saturday evenings. It was a large theatre with a complete semi-circle of boxes extending from one side to the other. The centre one, called the 'Royal' or 'Omnibus' was available for a comparatively small charge (I think less than two pounds). It had ten seats, so Frank who disliked plays, but was quite fond of comedy turns, booked it most Saturday nights for us all. This often-included mixed company and I was invited to include an occasional girlfriend.

Frank had developed a warm relationship with the manager of 'The Mitre' and his wife, through mid-week visits there and as the pub was shut at weekends they would be included in the party to the Stoll. The usual practice was for the men to leave the ladies in the box while they, intermittently, adjourned to the bar for most of the show; everyone gathering, however, to see and hear the last act, 'the top of the bill'. This was, invariably, some of the leading comedians of the period, notably Max Miller, Ted Ray, Vic Oliver and the Crazy Gang, amongst many others.

John and Mary, the Mitre couple, would then invite some of us back to their inn for a private supper in their rooms, up above the closed bar. As food was getting very scarce (for instance, we were allowed only one egg per month), and generally lacking in variety, such meals, as only publicans could stretch their reserves to make attractive, were extremely welcome. At about midnight Frank and I, waving our thanks to our hosts, would wend our way back to the basement at Goldsmith Building to continue our thirst-quenching operations by attacking the Watney's, making sure to leave a couple of bottles for VH the following evening.

It is a pity that the Stoll was done away with. Whether it was just allowed to close down because of lack of patronage after the War I cannot say. The site is now an office block.

I have one vibrant memory of our visits to the theatre. As usual, we had pressed our luck a little too far. One Saturday evening, we were enjoying our customary 'truant' visit there when, above the noise of a singing and dancing act, we heard what sounded like thunder. Convinced that it was a heavy storm, we continued with our enjoyment in the box or bar. When we got outside, we were stunned to see the sky bright red and incendiaries cascading all around us. With great haste we ran back to find that the Temple was getting its share of fire bombs.

Halfway down Middle Temple Lane, we saw the dishevelled figure of Gwillam, covered in muck and sweat, shaking a clenched fist at us and, very rightly, demanding to know where we had been. Quick as a flash, Frank lied that we had been running all over the Temple putting sandbags over the bombs and searching for our leader, but that we had somehow missed him. Perhaps it was Frank's gift of the gab or of his beer, which persuaded him to believe this most unlikely story. Suffice it to say that we were extremely lucky not to be severely reprimanded for our dereliction of duty.

I was very pleased, however, to discover that miraculously no fires actually broke out in the Temple on that particular night, unlike on many others when the City was peppered with this detestable form of warfare.

Poor old Gwillam had a wretched job really. Being the Head Porter, he lived in one of the basements opposite the Inner Temple Hall (later totally destroyed). He was, therefore, always 'on the job' and as far as I know, had to act whether he liked it or not, as the Chief Fire Warden seven nights a week.

The heaviest bombing of the City took place on Sunday nights. It always seemed to be on Monday morning, after walking from Temple Station along the Embankment and up Middle Temple Lane, that I found the debris of high explosive and fire damage apparent all around.

The route through to Goldsmith Building was often a diversion via Fleet Street or Tudor Street because the heart of the Temple had suffered yet again. On one occasion, in early 1941, the Cloisters and, just a few yards away, Lamb Building, were completely demolished by bombs. The damage also extended to part of the nearby Temple Church. I have a clear mental picture of the sad scene. Frank and I went to investigate and found Adam and one or two junior barristers surveying the depressing sight before them. Just a few yards away, Mr. F.W. Beney, an able contemporary of VH, and head of his own chambers, was similarly endeavouring to salvage anything worth saving from the heaps of rubble, which a few hours earlier had been Lamb Building.

We supplied coffee to them all and invited them back to chambers where we did our best to console them. F.W. Beney was immediately offered a share of our rooms. This was extended to his team, which were his colleague Gilbert Dare, his clerk Sid Ashby, and his typist Mrs. Royds. All of them were given the room previously occupied by John Senter and Helenas Milmo. Although very cramped, it was very gratefully accepted.

St. John Field, or whoever was the most influential remaining member of the Cloisters set, managed to get some alternative accommodation in Lincoln's Inn, almost at once. It was to be about eight months before F.W. Beney got other premises and for this he had to move out of his beloved Inner Temple and take over a few odd rooms in Garden Court, under the auspices of the Middle Temple.

Meanwhile they stayed with us at Goldsmith Building where I got to know them very well. It was desirable, however, that while we shared things like telephones in the clerks' room and the waiting room, we remained two separate sets of chambers.

It was about this time that we suffered badly at home. The first main attack on London took place in September 1940, a year after War broke out, and it was the East End which took the brunt. This was because of the attempt to knock out the nearby London Docks.

I vividly recall standing on a fairly high bridge in Campbell Road, Bow, one night on my way home and watching with total and unbeliev-able amazement, the panoramic scene of the inferno as the Docks burned. On this night, and for most thereafter, we slept fully in the Anderson Shelter, which at best held four people horizontally.

We were then subjected to almost constant air raids. The shelter was proof against anything but a direct hit, though it did nothing to muffle the noise of the planes and bombs, and later the anti-aircraft guns.

Every day, after an overnight raid, we learned of houses being wiped out barely a hundred yards from our home and of the number of people killed and wounded. It was like Russian roulette. Ultimately it happened.

Suddenly one night the ground shook so much we thought that our end had finally come. A string of bombs, not very large, were dropped along Fairfoot Road, one knocking down the house opposite ours, as a direct hit. Although one or two people were killed some way along the road, the shelters saved many others, but the blast extended across to us and we were very effectively 'bombed out'. All the ceilings were destroyed and the woodwork of doors and window frames torn out with most of the contents damaged. We had to move and quickly!

My mother, as may be expected, reported our plight to the Little Sisters of the Assumption in Wellington Way. True to form the good nuns came to our rescue in allowing us to take over and rent one of two vacant houses which they owned right next to their convent.

Ten Wellington Way was a huge, four storey semi-detached house, which had seen better days earlier in the century, the road being then one of the 'in' areas in Bow. In fact, George Lansbury, the 'father' of the Labour Party owned a house there a couple of decades before.

Unfortunately, there was no Anderson Shelter in the garden. It is true that there was a basement which could be converted into some kind of protection, but we considered it much less safe than what we had been used to, so we continued to go back most evenings to Fairfoot Road which was about half a mile away, and sleep in our old garden shelter.

It took a few days for my father and I to move our remaining goods and chattels with the aid of a pushcart, it being impossible to hire or procure a van for the purpose.

The indomitable spirit was not impaired in the slightest degree by these setbacks either within the family or generally! No one appeared to have lost their faith in final victory. This, of course, did not mean that we were not pretty scared with the bombing, but whereas I, with the impetuosity of youth, would stupidly stand out in the open and gape at the happenings above us in the sky, my mother grew more and more afraid, especially after our bad blasting.

She finally had to get well away from the noise and made enquiries about getting down and sleeping in the Tube. Many others had the same idea, so much so that in seeking a permanent spot on a deep Underground station, my mother could not get a berth nearer than Marble Arch – about nine or ten stations away on the Central Line. She persuaded a friend to join her there. They had assigned to them an area of about six feet by two feet each, which was chalk marked out on the platform with their reserved number. Occasionally I helped her down there with her blankets and personal effects. It wasn't very pleasant and I was glad to get back up on top, but it was at least better for my mother than the terrible fear of the exposure to bombing at ground level.

Once again, one could not fail to be impressed with the cheerfulness and sense of humour of all concerned. To pass the time, singsongs became a nightly feature.

TALES OF A BARRISTERS' CLERK

During the next few months, the bombing took its effect upon Central London. One of the most picturesque Temple buildings, Crown Office Row, disappeared overnight. It was the victim of a huge landmine, and as usual it was a Sunday night. Although not much more than fifty yards away, VH slept right through it! He needed only three or four hours of sleep, but heard not a whisper!

The building had four very attractive entrances surrounded by creeper. It is to be regretted that, whilst some of the bombed buildings were restored more or less to their original facade (such as Pump Court and the Cloisters), Crown Office Row was not, more's the pity! Over a third of the Temple was destroyed or severely damaged. But Goldsmith Building had a charmed life – at most it suffered an odd shattered pane of glass.

During 1941 as we did our best to cope with and adapt to the dramatic and unexpected pressures, the time was approaching when my age group for conscription would be reached. By mid-1941 I had received notice of call-up, together with an instruction to attend a London centre for a medical examination. I also had to choose which service I desired. I went for the RAF for no apparent reason (certainly not to become a Brylcreem Boy – my receding forehead did not lend itself to it), and was duly accepted, but in what capacity had yet to be determined.

When VH heard that I was soon to be on my way he applied to the RAF for my call up to be deferred. He pleaded that as Treasury Counsel, he was on essential Government work (which was true) and that as one of his depleted staff I was indispensable (which wasn't so true). He managed, nevertheless, to get a six months delay to my leaving. Then, because I was considered physically fit, no further concession was possible.

VH then tried to get me transferred as a clerk to the Judge Advocate General's Department, centred in London. Had that been possible, I could have maintained a close link with chambers, if it suited VH and Frank, working perhaps an hour or two in the evenings or on Saturdays. I do not think there was anything laid down in the regulations why this would not be possible, as long as one performed one's military duties first. Or maybe the authorities would not know about any unofficial help given anyway. I recall that serving barristers stationed in London were permitted to continue with their practice in their spare time or during leave, and that they sometimes appeared in court not in robes, but in uniform.

That alternative, however, was denied me for the same reason that deferment was rejected. I had to go on active service, clerking being one of the heads of the RAF group reserved for those not fully physically fit. I did not mind in the slightest once the position was clear.

I eventually had to report to Cardington in March of 1942. A few weeks earlier, when it was apparent that my civilian days were numbered, Frank decided that it would be a short-sighted policy to replace me with a male junior because of the probability of losing him too quickly through conscription.

He said that he thought he had the solution. An attractive outdoor solicitors' clerk named Maureen, who worked for Herbert Baron and Co., used to deliver papers occasionally to chambers and had caught Frank's eye. She was about 19 years old, with a very lively disposition and what was more important, laughed at our jokes (even when they were repeated!). When next she called in, Frank tackled her about working for chambers and she accepted even before he had finished the explanation of what she was expected to do, and that it was for the duration only.

She gave notice at once and within a few days was with us, overlapping with me for about eight weeks during which time she learned very quickly the ramifications of the ledgers, diary and how to deal with the clients. She was very efficient and had flair.

It was soon apparent that Frank's idea was a good one and that if he had any qualms about being left without proper assistance after I left, Maureen would soon dispel them. Furthermore she had two other outstanding points which could not be ignored!

During the four years that I had worked at Goldsmith Building, as is apparent, I had got on very well with Frank Connett. He had taught me most of what I know of clerking and how to get a good laugh out of circumstances surrounding the job. We had become good friends and never had a cross word throughout our association, including our weekly fire watching exploits. He took pains to make it clear that after the War, he wanted me to come back as his number two.

"Maureen understands that she is only here until you get back and with all the other barristers returning we will be a very powerful set of chambers. I will certainly need you."

Whilst that was very reassuring I was rather disturbed to hear Frank say, when I enquired as to where John Robertshaw would stand in the scheme, that he did not rank him a true barristers' clerk and that he should seek another type of job on his return. Whether that was true, only time would tell!

I was given a great send off. VH promised, as he had done for John Robertshaw, to subscribe ten shillings a week to my credit until I got back. This was fully honoured! He, Arthur Beecroft, Frank and a couple of pupils took me to dinner at Oddeninos, where I was presented with a very nice gold wrist watch. I felt sad leaving them, but it was quite a memorable occasion and got me off on the right footing.

CHAPTER SIX
Tom goes to war

More sad, of course, was saying farewell to the family. My father, unlike my mother, was not usually one for open sentimentality but was now rather emotional and gave me a great deal of advice. This was mainly directed at my survival.

We had become quite close, trying to cope with the bombing and easing my mother's state of nerves, but both of them felt that now the last of their brood was off, a certain loneliness would creep in. The real unspoken worry was, of course, that no-one could say when we would all be gathered safely together again.

I had saved £10 which I tucked away in my wallet as a safeguard against that 'rainy day'. With a heavy heart I said my 'goodbyes' and went off to the RAF station at Cardington, in Bedfordshire. It was the first time I had ever been away from home, apart from an odd week or two camping earlier on.

With my friends not around, the feeling of going into a totally unknown existence for an unspecified period of time was extremely depressing. But, fortunately, on the train from King's Cross I soon found other 'loners' and, typical of this kind of encounter, we all fell into an immediate close association as if we had been friends from birth. The main topic of chatter was an exchange of views about the options we would expect to be offered by way of service! Would we prefer air crew to ground staff? What of the chances of going overseas? Would we really have a choice?

On arrival, we were shunted from one hut to another, with endless delays at all of them, filling in forms and being physically examined again! We were kitted out with our uniform and given some general

149

orders about discipline and lectured on how to be good airmen at all times. The most galling experience was having to stand to attention in line and react quickly to the sergeant or corporal in charge. One or two of the 'gang' made a few vain attempts to retain their civilian status a little longer, by ignoring the orders or obeying them slowly and lethargically, but this hostility did not last long.

Loud bellowing by the non-commissioned officers soon put the 'fear of God' into us and we found, reluctantly, that acquiescence was the quickest way to 'peace and quiet'.

Then came the moment of truth. We went before the Selection Board to sort out our future! We all sat in a large cold hut or hanger, like a huge dentist's waiting room and were called into an inner area a few at a time, to be dispersed in various directions. The interviews lasted quite a few minutes. Finally my turn came. I was shown through two or three doors into a small room, where behind a trestle table, sat a solitary RAF sergeant. He was the 'Selection Board'. We had thought, erroneously, that there would be at least four or five 'big-wigs'.

His greeting was not unkind. In a hushed voice, he requested me, before sitting down on the only other chair facing him across the desk to: "Just look to see if anyone is listening at the door please." I looked and reported that there was not. "Good," said he; "You will see that the window is closed. This is because what I have to say to you is in the most secret confidence. Parsliffe, I have been looking here at your qualifications (although there didn't seem to be much data before him) and I feel that you are the type of chap we're looking for." He went on: "I will say this only once! We have a secret weapon which will probably win us the War sooner than we had expected. It has been kept a closely guarded secret. Churchill has only recently been informed, and not many other people, even in high office, know about it. Tell me, Parsliffe, have you ever heard of (and here he spoke in a mere whisper) "Radiolocation"?

"Never," said I, catching my breath dramatically.

"That is as well," said he. "If you had, something would be drastically wrong".

I was beginning to become quite intrigued with the turn of events.

I had the distinct feeling that this NCO, along with Churchill, a few top scientists and now me, were the only ones in on something rather historically wonderful.

"The invention, just developed, is to send a radio wave out from a transmitter into the sky." He went on quietly "We know the direction it is going – and when it strikes an aircraft, it is reflected back and picked up by a huge receiver. We then halve the distance it has travelled and the result is that we know the position of the enemy plane."

"Gosh," said I, not knowing what other mark of astonishment would be appropriate.

He continued: "Simple, though it sounds, Germany has not yet got it, and we have, therefore, an immense advantage over them with this one! Tell me, Parsliffe, are you with us?"

"Yes, Sergeant," said I with some enthusiasm.

"Good – I must impress upon you that this must be kept entirely to yourself. When you go home on leave eventually, not a hint to your family – and when you join your colleagues in a moment or two, not a hint to them either. If they ask you what you have joined, just tell them 'Sorry, I am not allowed to say'. I want your word on this."

"You have it, Sergeant" I replied.

"Good, you will receive further instructions very soon. Please go now and re-join your squad." said he.

When I got back to my new found friends, they asked: "What have you been pushed into?"

"Sorry, chaps, I cannot say." said I.

"So, you've been landed with Radiolocation just like the rest of us! Welcome," they said.

So 'Radar' (as it was soon to be called) it was! But first, the discipline.

We were despatched, via Warrington to Blackpool for 'square bashing' which meant drill, physical training and the total surrender to accepting orders without question. In white vests, black shorts and slippers, we ran up and down the sands until we could have dropped – not a very attractive sight!

I was billeted in a typical Blackpool landlady's boarding house – how they cashed in on the RAF! We were three or four to a small bedroom and the food was abysmal – not much more than potatoes served in various ways. So much so, that we had to augment this 'nourishment' with fish and chips every night. We were grateful to find that this particular fare was both plentiful and cheap in the town.

We were paid only about one and sixpence or one and ninepence a day, but with that restricted amount and despite the 10.30 p.m. curfew, which was rigorously applied, we were able to hit the town in a big way. The Tower Ballroom, Winter Gardens and many other places of entertainment we took in our stride!

We saw 'Wakes Week' where a town tends to move en masse to the seaside every summer, in operation at close quarters. It seemed surprising that this north country practise continued in Wartime, when one would suppose the factories would be kept going non-stop.

Although blacked-out and despite the appalling landladies, it was a most enjoyable place to spend three months, even though the summer of 1942 was not a good one for sunny or warm weather. I recall one discordant event – we were lined up as a squad on the promenade one morning as usual. The Sergeant went through his 'I will play ball with you, if you play ball with me,' routine, followed by the rollcall. The procedure was that he would shout out the last three digits of our service number, followed by our surname. The airman would then answer: "Here, Sergeant". On this particular day, one of our number was absent through sickness. The dialogue went something like this:

NCO: "382 Roberts". "Here Sergeant".

NCO: "965 Williams". "Here Sergeant".

NCO: "374 Parsliffe". "Here Sergeant".

NCO: "761 Futcher". Nothing.

NCO: "I repeat, 761 Futcher". Nothing.

NCO: (Louder): "761 Futcher". Still nothing.

At this point a friend and I could not resist the comment:

(In unison) "There ain't no FUTURE in the Air Force, Sergeant!"

This was greeted with hoots of laughter from the rest of the squad, but not our sergeant. We were all punished with extra duties for two or three days.

The NCOs no doubt did their job well, but they totally lacked humour and did not endear themselves to us as a whole! And yet we presented our chap with a small present after we had passed out at the end of this period of our training, which meant he could not have been all bad.

After a short leave home, we were instructed to report next to the technical course at Yatesbury in Wiltshire. After Blackpool this was a most boring place. The camp had nothing to commend it, being miles from any town.

We sat earnestly around trainee cathode ray tubes and tried to decipher the dots and traces which were the means of plotting enemy planes. No one seemed happy with their choice of trade, even if Churchill might be pleased with us. With no great enthusiasm we eventually passed the appropriate level of the tests, which meant we were now radar operators and referred to as 'technical personnel'. This title was a source of much criticism and unnecessary friction between some of the personnel of the various RAF trades.

I, for one, could not truthfully be described as 'technical' to the slightest degree and it was not at all necessary anyway to be such in order to operate the radar tubes. Radar 'mechanics' were the real people who deserved that label. It was ludicrous that motor mechanics and drivers, amongst others, were classified as 'non-technical'. It seemed that anyone having anything to do with Radar was described as 'technical' – but was not.

This farcical situation reached its most absurd when, sometime later in the Middle East, mobile Radar units were formed with two officers. The senior ranking one, being the Commanding Officer, was responsible for all his staff and the safety of the unit; the other, appropriately trained, being in charge of the 'operational side'. The latter was deemed to be technical and the former was not! Also, because Radar was regarded as very secret, the Commanding Officer, despite being the 'boss' was unbelievably banned, officially at any rate, from entering his lorries which housed the transmitter and receiver and observing the success or otherwise of our endeavours.

After Yatesbury, we were split up into groups of three or four and sent all over the country to Radar stations, most of which were on the south or east costs facing occupied Europe. I got Whitstable, in the mouth of the Thames, as my posting. This was a good assignment, so far as I was concerned. Although the town was not very lively, we were in private billets, much better than Blackpool, with more friendly landladies. There was no curfew and the RAF personnel at the station took over the Long Reach Tavern, just around the corner by Thanet Way, as our 'club' or substitute for a NAAFI.

This met with the proprietor's approval because, as Whitstable was within the three-mile coastal restriction, there were no tourists and along with a few locals we kept him in business.

We had 'mixed company' with WAAFS being an integral part of the station staff. In my opinion, women were far better than men in 'reading the radar screens' and were much neater in plotting the planes on the tables in the filter rooms

Another great plus was that we were on a 'four-watch' system, which gave us quite a lot of free time. I managed to get a 36-hour pass about once a fortnight, and hitchhiked my way home, being no more than about 60-miles away.

We had arrived in Whitstable in mid-September, and quickly became part of the social scene. Everyone made us welcome and encouraged us to join in the heavy preparations for a great Christmas. As far as the operations were concerned, not forgetting that we were there for that purpose, a number of German planes were plotted by us in their intermittent raids on London, although the Battle of Britain had long since been won.

For just a day or two, a few of us were transferred to the much larger Radar station at Dover, a few miles south. This was probably Britain's number one, being the closest installation to France. I was proud, when asked one night, to be the operator on the main tube for an hour as the 'eyes' of Britain. The limit of our range was something up to 200 miles into Europe. I would like to be able to say that I plotted dozens of German planes flying around the Channel, but in fact it was one of the quietest periods of the night and nothing at all appeared on the screen.

Just when we were getting down to the fine tuning of our Michaelmas plans (for instance, we had in mind putting on a pantomime), and to generally having a good time, news came through that the 'Yatesbury' boys were to be posted to Worth Matravers in Dorset, in preparation for overseas service. It was a most severe body blow, especially as we had to move on December 21st. We were told that in no way could it be delayed.

Having arrived at what appeared to be 'Wuthering Heights' in blinding rain and on top of a dangerous cliff in the dark, we were left with no instructions for over a week and Christmas was by far the worst I have ever experienced – even the NAAFI shut early.

Eventually we underwent all the paraphernalia of special training and medication for overseas. It was not until April 1943 that we sailed, in the Polish ship 'Sobieski' from Gourock in the Clyde. After a circuitous route around the Atlantic, to avoid 'U' boats, we arrived eventually at Durban, in South Africa.

As the War in the Mediterranean was gradually and successfully coming to an end we became the last large convoy to go round the Cape of Good Hope on our way to the Middle East. We stayed in that attractive town for about a week before going up the east coast, disembarking finally at Port Tufik at the southern end of the Suez Canal.

Because we had landed on African soil three days before the last German or Italian was pushed into the sea thousands of miles away in Tunisia, we were later awarded a medal, the 'Africa Star'!

We were taken to a place called Helwan, twenty miles from Cairo, where we underwent a further course of radar training. After a while we were formed up into small mobile units for dispatch around the Middle East area including Palestine, Syria and the Lebanon and this entailed many journeys across the Sinai desert!

Whenever we settled on an appropriate site and had got operational, after a week or two we were ordered to dismantle our equipment and get back to base. We then stagnated for a few weeks in the sandy wastes of Helwan playing bridge, trying to avoid sunstroke, and getting utterly bored until the next posting. Each time we got ourselves organised, we had to return.

These charades were due to the stark fact that as the War had moved on into Italy and Greece, there was no enemy to deal with! Only once did we make our mark. It was when operating from the top of Mount Carmel, overlooking Haifa and 'covering' the eastern Mediterranean we suddenly picked up one night, a large 'echo' on our Radar tube. This indicated that about 20 unidentified aircraft were approaching Palestine from, a point only fifty miles away. Fitter Rook, to whom we hurriedly passed this vital information, got themselves into a panic and stayed that way for quite a while, until some other units (I think it was the Observer Corps) reported that a large flight of birds had been sighted making its way eastwards. I suppose it is not altogether surprising, that sometimes the feathered variety also respond faithfully to a well-intended wave!

The last excursion into a totally non-productive situation was when, with three or four other small units, we were sent off in an LCT vessel, via Cyprus, en route to set up 'shop' on the Greek island of Kos, in the Dodecanese. At last it seemed we would be doing something useful. Alas, the Germans, who had been kicked out of the islands some days before, unexpectedly re-invaded and re-took possession.

We were told to get the hell out of the area and back to Egypt yet again as quickly as possible. Although British forces regained Kos fairly soon, the impetus had gone. It was, I believe, the last Allied withdrawal of the Mediterranean war and no further attempt was made within the Middle East command to use us gainfully or at all! We were left to rot in Helwan.

Thank goodness for Bridge – after a short formal parade, I played all day, every day, occasionally going into Cairo with my partner to vary our efforts at one or two of the recognised Service Clubs with card rooms. Some people went 'sand happy' – a form of temporary mental paralysis caused by endless days of nothing but clear skies and the incessant sun beating down on the reflective sand which surrounded us. We yearned for the only two days of rain which drop on Egypt every January, with the predictability of Halley's Comet. But when it duly arrived we found it cold and depressing, so acclimatised had we become to the extreme heat.

After what seemed an eternity, we heard news 'on the grapevine' that massive Radar postings were imminent in the Italian theatre of War, following the Allied successes there. About 95% of our strength was involved – I was amongst the 5% that remained, kept back, so it seemed, as a token reserve for the Middle East, or even the Far East, had the War there not been brought to an abrupt end the following year with the dropping of the Atomic Bomb!

CHAPTER SEVEN

They also serve who only stand and wait

With so many comrades transferred to the European campaign, life in Helwan became more and more bleak, with the game of Bridge the main reason I did not go 'sand happy'. The War seemed very far away, as did the UK and home.

I was grateful for the continuous stream of letters from my mother in which she expressed herself in the same excitable way that she would orally describe events. This was mostly a series of unrelated comments about everything surrounding her life in Bow.

By contrast, my father, with his less regular communications, displayed a better appreciation of what might appear interesting to me. He was right on course in describing the War and how he thought it might be won. He had very neat handwriting and expressed himself in a most pleasant way. It is quite amazing that through the medium of the written word, he revealed his character far more convincingly than when face to face at home. I had no idea how literary he could be, and began to look forward eagerly to his letters. It was unfortunate that my drab existence did not lend itself to a flow of pungent news items in return.

Not for the first time my thoughts turned to the Temple and Goldsmith Building in particular. Although I received an occasional letter from Maureen, with a postscript from Frank, I found it difficult to envisage how life was progressing there and what changes may have taken place. Doubts started to creep into my daydreaming as to whether I was really cut out for the unique Temple way of life and what alternatives might be feasible, brought about, I suspect, by the extreme circumstances in which I found myself. But with the lethargy that is generated by this form of inactivity, the decision could be shelved until a later date.

Meanwhile something had to be done about the intolerable boredom. I had an acquaintance, Norman Surridge, who had got himself a job of sorts at the RAF Middle East command in the heart of Cairo. We occasionally met in town for a game of cards, there being no appropriate female company around to excite our masculinity. One day he announced that although I was not a clerk by RAF classification, he thought he could 'fix' it for me to be posted into the Signals Section at Headquarters for general office duties, because they had apparently got a shortage of staff there.

With no hope of promotion in Radar or of getting 're-mustered' (officially to change one's trade grouping), I jumped at the opportunity to become more occupied than I had hitherto been. Besides Cairo was a fairly lively place in which to be stationed.

Norman was as good as his word and a week later I was transferred to Kubri Camp, right next to the then titled 'English' Bridge over the Nile, in the centre of the city. Ironically, I arrived half way through the annual downpour of January (1945) and because there was no great lasting need for drains, I had to wade through inches of flood water to get to my test, assisted by a friendly corporal, who I later learned was the camp 'gay'.

In the office, I was put in charge of the records of all signals personnel in the command, under the direction of an officer called Webb. He was responsible for the distribution and movement of such airmen, particularly those involved with the busy Transport Command stations dotted across the Middle East, as a link between the UK and the Far East. These were mainly Wireless Operators and Mechanics – Radar becoming less and less required the further the War had moved away. Webb was also the effective guardian of their personal problems and became the arbiter of, for example, compassionate postings home in the event of family disasters and the like.

One airman, a wireless operator, put in a strong plea, that far from being repatriated, he should be allowed to remain in Egypt for an indeterminate period of time. When we looked into his history we found that the poor fellow had, a few weeks earlier, received a 'Dear John' letter from his long time fiancée in England, informing him that she had met and fallen for an American G.l. serving close by.

He was so crestfallen that he made advances (clearly on the rebound) to a female 'fellahein' who had crossed his path recently near where he was serving, just outside Cairo. She came from the lowest Arab social order (class distinction being as wide in that part of the Middle East as anywhere). She was the type who dressed in long black clothes, wore a yashmak and was heavily accompanied by flies buzzing around her wherever she went. How he met her or managed civilised contact was a mystery. But he got a proposal going and was accepted. All that was required, under service regulations, was the CO's permission to marry and this was passed on to my boss for consideration as part of his moral responsibilities.

In the circumstances he instantly refused and authorised me to put in motion an immediate posting for the wretched man, as far away as possible for his own good. This was done, but within a comparatively short time, as was now the pattern with the ever-shrinking command, the unit was disbanded and he was returned to base – an experience with which I was all too familiar. Two or three times he was sent off to faraway places, only to be brought back soon to within fraternisation contact with his 'beloved', on each occasion renewing his request to wed. Finally Flight Lieutenant Webb announced that he was fed up playing 'God'. He said: 'Who am I to say that he cannot marry this woman? He's a grown man and has been very persistent. Let him have his way!'

Official permission, ultimately and painfully thus obtained, the wedding took place, although we were not invited. I can only hope that they remained happy!

As we moved through 1945 a lot of people, having served abroad for three years (if married) and four years (if not), were repatriated. It had become the practice for the fortunate persons to throw a farewell party a few days before departure home and for that purpose, the senior Signals officer, an Air Vice Marshall, allowed the use of his big conference room, on the clear understanding that all ranks, himself included, were invited. The main fare, apart from peanuts and sausages on sticks, was Cypriot brandy and bottles of 'Stella' beer, the latter being kept cool by being immersed in ice in a large dustbin. The celebrations usually started at about 7 p.m. and lasted as long as the drinks held out. They were very enjoyable and eventually took place two or three evenings a week.

The Air Vice Marshal was most charming and mixed freely with the junior officers and other ranks. He got to know us all very well. Towards the end of 1945, on one such occasion, he came over to socialise with a group of us airmen and enquired of me, en passant, where I hailed from and was I a member of a large family. I explained that I was born in London and had three sisters and a brother.

"Is your brother in the RAF, Parsliffe?" he asked.

"No, Sir," said I. "He is in the Army, serving as a Sapper in the Royal Engineers in Greece."

"When did you last see him?" asked the AVM. I replied, "Over three years ago, Sir. As a matter of fact he is getting married to a local girl in Salonika in a few days' time." (Jack had apparently managed to get his CO's consent fairly quickly, without being posted away first).

The conversation continued:

AVM: "That is very interesting, Parsliffe. Tell me, is your family going over for the Wedding?"

Me: "No, Sir," (with a chuckle) "There is a War on. They wouldn't be allowed to, of course!"

AVM: "Quite so, I forgot! Why don't you go?"

Me: "I'd love to Sir, but how can I? It's a different Command and anyway I have no leave due."

AVM: "Such difficulties are made to be overcome, Parsliffe. Come to see me in my room tomorrow morning, when we both will be more sober and we will discuss it further, OK?

Me: "Certainly, Sir-thank you!"

I thought about this overnight, but decided that the AVM was just being kind with his chatter and would, in all probability, not wish to revive the discussion. I could not have been more wrong. Ten minutes after arriving for duty early next day I had a call on the 'intercom' that the AVM wanted to see me at once. After knocking on the door and entering his room the discourse went along these lines:

AVM: "There you are, Parsliffe – what kept you?"

Before I could answer, he went on: "I know that you are not a clerk – what is your real trade?"

Me: "Radar, Sir."
AVM: "Good! I propose to ask my friend, AVM Foley, who is my opposite number in Athens, to request the urgent need for a Radar specialist for a speedy visit to RAF Station Salonika. I will write him a personal note along these lines. When I get his reply I will send for you again. It was a good night, last night, wasn't it? Goodbye for now."

Thanking him once more, I took my leave, wondering what the outcome would be. Scarcely 24 hours later, he sent for me again and threw across the table for my perusal, a MOST URGENT signal from Athens which requested: 'As a matter of Top Priority', the immediate assistance of a Radar Technician to be attached for a short time to deal with complicated problems arising at RAF Station, Salonika.'

"Now Parsliffe," said the AVM: "Where can we find a Radar man at such short notice with so many of them up in Italy at this time?"

"Sir" said I,"I have been trained as a Radar Operator – do you think I could volunteer?"

"Indeed you can. That's the spirit! I'll forward your name and off you go! Give my regards to your brother and wish him well for the future. Don't hang around too long after the ceremony; try to be back within a week or so, there's a good chap."

But what if they don't believe the real reason for the trip, Sir?" I asked. "Good point," he replied. "I will give you a demi-official: 'To Whom It May Concern' note explaining the need for you to be allowed to attend your brother's wedding. That should do the trick. Don't disclose it unless anyone in authority over there doubts your story."

He soon produced a letter and waved me on my way. I could not thank him enough. I had no time to get a message through to Jack, because appropriate arrangements having been rushed through, I was soon enjoying a top priority marking for travel to Greece.

There were only about five other people on the afternoon Dakota flight to Athens, all of them high ranking officers from all three services. They regarded me, a mere LAC, with some suspicion, but no questions were asked. After changing planes at Athens, I flew over the mountains to RAF Station, Salonika.

On arrival, at about 8 p.m., I was shown into the Orderly Room and eventually into the CO's office. He was a Squadron Leader and looked far from happy. He wasted no words on warm greetings: "What on earth are you doing here? According to the signal I've received you are a specialist who is going to put our non-existent Radar equipment into good operational order. Tell me, what's it all about?" I regaled him with the full story, his mouth dropping open more and more as I proceeded.

"Does anyone in the Middle East know that we have recently been engaged in a fierce war up here in north Greece? In any event, I find your story most unlikely to be true – I just don't believe it, Parsliffe!"

It was time for the letter. He read it through three times before asking in a weary voice and with a resigned expression:

"When is your brother getting married?"

"In two days' time, Sir" said I.

"We are very much undermanned on this unit. If you are officially attached to us for a few days, the least I must ask you to do, apart from going to the wedding, is to perform a few duties. I suggest you take the shift on the telephone exchange tonight for starters and we will sort out your personal requirements tomorrow."

"Very good Sir" said I.

163

Although tired after the flight, I fully understood his incredulous attitude. Everyone on the station seemed to be war-worn and depressed, something I had not experienced at all in the Middle East. I must confess that I felt a bit mean. The switchboard was exactly like the one we had back in chambers and, as such, was no problem. The difficulty was in understanding the Greek which from time to time came flooding through on some of the calls.

Towards the end of the watch (at about 7 a.m.) I had learned enough to get some idea of how to get through to the local Army Unit where I assumed Jack would be stationed. After a long series of linkups I managed to contact the guard room of the Royal Engineers, and although experiencing some difficulty in getting the point across to the NCO in charge, Sapper John Parsliffe was duly aroused from his slumbers to take a call in the guard room. Thinking that the line to Cairo was particularly clear, it took him some time to realise that I was just up the road and looking forward eagerly to meeting him and his prospective bride. It was a great moment. Within an hour or two we had met and talked incessantly about everything, but mainly about how I had come to be in Salonika in this way. I met his fiancée, a beautiful girl called Nitsa, who belonged to one of the respected families in the town, her father being a dentist.

The wedding took place the next day and I was Jack's best man. The reception was held in Nitsa's parents' home. Unfortunately, not being able to speak any Greek I was unable to talk as much as I would have liked to my new sister-in-law who only knew a few scant words of English. I did gather, however, that Jack had given her the impression that we all lived in abodes similar to the Park Lane apartments portrayed in the Anna Neagle and Michael Wilding films shown there at the time!

The drink supplied was, inevitably, ouzo – but as the padre duly warned, it was then stark wood alcohol and best avoided. Although Jack had got some leave it was impossible for him and his wife to go away on honeymoon – there was no place to go! The War had taken a heavy toll of the town and surrounding areas, and there was the unmistakable depression which accompanies such tragedies.

Having spent one more most enjoyable evening in the company of the newlyweds and the family, I thought it time to leave them and get back fairly soon to Egypt, after perhaps looking round Athens en route. I had been treated with nothing but warmth and kindness over the three days and, subject to getting clearance from the RAF Station, I said my goodbyes interspersed with a shower of kisses all round.

It would have been an abuse of the AVM's trust to hang about in Greece for any length of time even if I had wanted to do so! I therefore returned to the airbase and requested the CO, to terminate my attachment to his unit and clear me to board a plane back. I found his attitude quite different from our earlier encounter. He could not be more friendly and confided in me that he was absolutely fed up to the back teeth with Greece and the smell of War. He asked me quite frankly if, on my return to Headquarters in Cairo, I could persuade the AVM to effect a posting for him the other way round. He was desperate to enjoy the sunshine and the settled lifestyle which was now available in the Middle East. I promised to do what I could.

He gave me the necessary release and at nine o'clock the next morning, I boarded the only plane that flew daily between Salonika and Athens. We were just about to take off when the landing wheel was found to be unserviceable. We had to disembark while the fault was investigated. After a long delay, it was reported that a spare would have to be flown up from Athens which meant the flight would be postponed until the following day. The CO was very co-operative and suggested that I rejoin my brother meanwhile.

The greetings were eagerly renewed by everyone and another pleasant evening was spent with Nitsa's parents at their home, culminating in more goodbyes and another round of kisses. "We will wave as we see the plane go off tomorrow – have a pleasant trip," were the final words of encouragement.

The next day, however, on reporting for take-off I was told that the weather had deteriorated so much over the mountains that there would again be no flight. I therefore offered my services at the RAF Station and the CO found me a few duties to 'justify' my attachment before going off duty later in the day. Back with Jack and the in-laws, for another evening, we did our best to maintain the novelty of the occasion finishing up with the usual farewell endearments!

For three more days, something was wrong with the plane or the weather, and the pattern was repeated. Finally the good folk declined to proffer their kisses, convinced that I would be back yet again the following day. Inevitably the next day's departure was a success and I flew gratefully to Athens.

Had there been no delays at Salonika I might have stayed over in the capital for a day or two, but in the circumstances I was anxious to get back to Egypt. I reported to AVM who was pleased to hear about the wedding and amused to be told the story of the plane and the hold ups. After thanking him profusely for all that he had done, I did my best for the Salonika CO, but the AVM considered the suggestion impractical and beyond even his magical powers.

After experiencing in Greece just a little of what life was like after War had struck (very similar to one's feelings during the Blitz), I looked upon the tranquillity of Cairo in a somewhat different light. Working hours at Headquarters were about 8.30 a.m. to 1 p.m. and again between 5 p.m. and 7 p.m. This enabled me to relax, as a base-wallah, fairly fully. Apart from cards and repatriation parties, there was afternoon tennis at the fashionable Willcocks Sports Club, followed by tea on the verandah while watching cricket, before going back on duty in the evening!

The War had been won, first in Europe and then within three months in the Far East as well. There was nothing to stop our return home – obviously we were not needed in Egypt, a friendly country, as occupational troops, unlike enemy territory, where some would be required to be held back.

It would have been nice to be home for VJ day, but it was not to be. We were kept overseas much longer than most of us thought necessary. I suppose it was the same in other theatres of War, but in the Middle East it was the reason why so many servicemen withheld their support for Churchill, because repatriation was not quick enough. It was certainly one of the contributing factors in the downfall of the Conservative

Party, when after the defeat of Japan, the Prime Minister dissolved the National Government and called a general election.

Eventually my turn came and having observed the courtesy of throwing the conference room party and saying farewell to those who remained, not forgetting my friend, the Air Vice Marshal, I happily packed my kit for the journey home! I boarded a boat at Port Said and there met up with a mere handful of Radar people, the last in the Middle East, including my old Whitstable buddy, Les Whiting.

We sailed to Toulon on the French Riviera, where we spent a rather miserable two weeks awaiting a train to take us across France. The only exciting pastime in the town was endeavouring to avoid the service police in getting to the Out of Bounds area, where one or two shady exhibitions were staged at enormous expense.

At last, having travelled all night with very little sleep, we reached Calais and the Channel. A great cheer went up from us all when we sighted the White Cliffs of Dover from the ferry. After disembarking and kissing the ground, like the Pope, we were allowed into town for a two-hour break before boarding a further train to our UK destinations.

It was a mid-week lunchtime, which meant that the pubs were open. We raced to the nearest one and ordered pints of bitter, anxious to check the difference in strength between the 'Stella' chemical beer we had become used to in Egypt and that which was made with good old English hops. Alas we found that the home brew was extremely weak and had deteriorated greatly since we had been away. It was some time before it was restored to its earlier potency.

After a couple of days at Cardington, getting our UK status sorted out, we were released to go home for a period of repatriation leave. At last the end was in sight!

My War had really been a non-event, as far as fighting went! I had not fired a single shot in anger or actually seen a German or Italian antagonist. Was it sufficient to say: "They also serve who only stand and wait"? I had been infinitely more exposed during the bombing of London than at any time while in the forces and the only action I experienced was the plotting of some enemy planes at Whitstable. And yet, I felt that it had not all been in vain and I had, like almost everyone else, grown up a little. I had seen a bit of the world, which otherwise would not have been possible. I had become independent, and albeit with only a kit bag, had learnt to look after myself.

I was unable to notify home that I was on my way, it being some time before we got ourselves on the telephone, so my parents, along with the rest of the family, had no idea it was me as I rang the doorbell in Wellington Way. It was great to be home at last and to find that, apart from being just a little bit older, no one was apparently the worse for the intervening years and that they had well and truly survived it all.

Jack had got home before me but had to wait a while for permission from the authorities to bring Nitsa from Greece to England. They were particularly fastidious in checking that a proper home was available for her.

As it would not be more than a few weeks before I was finally demobilised I decided to visit the Temple during this leave and check what that might hold for me in the future. I had not heard in recent weeks from Maureen and was beginning to become just a little sceptical, as to whether the halcyon and encouraging remarks of Frank before my departure, would be recalled and renewed. However, despite any previous doubts, I had come to the conclusion that not being sufficiently trained in any other form of commercial subject, I was not in any position to contemplate other forms of employment even if I had wanted to.

My earlier civilian clothes did not quite fit me and the 'demob' suit would not be forthcoming until I actually finished service with the RAF. I had, therefore, to continue to wear my uniform. I felt every bit like a new boy again, as I climbed the two steps leading to the doorway of the ground floor Chambers of Valentine Holmes.

CHAPTER EIGHT

A rude awakening

Sometimes words are not necessary for a person to grasp an appreciation of an established fact. One look at Frank's face and to his reaction to my appearing in the doorway of the clerks room (I had long since learned the art of ducking) was enough for me to realise that things were decidedly different; even before his hand had been offered in greeting.

It did not surprise me that Maureen was very much in charge of the mechanics of the business in hand and looked solidly the second-in-command, but both were clearly nonplussed. Frank was standing with his back to the fireplace and was, unusually for him, momentarily silent.

I began to think that I should have warned him I was coming. Then, after the handshake and a pat on the back and faithful to his habits, he suggested that we adjourned to the 'Cock' for a chat over a homecoming drink.

Just at that moment, Robertshaw came into the room along with a new young junior or 'boy' called 'Ginger' Phipps, but it was plain all was not well. I knew then that there was no future for me in those chambers. John and I warmly renewed what had always been a genuine friendship with a quick exchange of items of news.

Frank was anxious to explain to me as soon as possible the events since I had left four years before, and after a quick welcome back from the great VH between conferences, we made our way to the pub. By now he had regained his composure and began by quickly stating that chambers were keen to retain the services of the efficient Maureen, despite what had been proposed in 1942 when she succeeded me for the 'duration'. But this had caused problems as soon as John had returned a few months earlier.

The regulations governing the re-employment of returning servicemen were quite clear. If the person so desired, the employer had to reinstate him (I believe for a minimum of one year), at not less than the outgoing level of income. John had insisted on coming back to the fold, but instead of being restored to his old desk position as the recognised first junior clerk (now fully occupied by Maureen) he was put in charge of the ledgers and fee-monitoring in our old shelter in the basement. The room had been converted into a second clerks room at the end of the War. This he shared with 'Ginger' and was understandably far from happy.

My sudden arrival further aggravated a most complicated situation. If, like John, I elected to jump aboard the bandwagon, an impossible state of affairs would be reached. I think Frank was sincere in saying that he would have liked our old partnership to be revived, but in the circumstances he immediately offered to find me a good second clerk's job elsewhere in the Temple with one of his many friends, if I so wished.

Just where I would have fitted into the embarrassing hierarchy under Connett, if I pressed my claim, would be hard to contemplate. I decided not to even try. I put Frank at his ease at once by saying that, as things appeared to stand in his clerks room, in any event I wanted none of it. This reply seemed to suffice and he suggested that between then and the final day of my discharge from the RAF he would 'lobby' his colleagues accordingly.

With the disbandment of some of the War time amalgamations and the rehabilitation of many returning barristers, sets of chambers were being re-organised and there were apparently some good junior jobs waiting to be filled.

I was, of course, deeply disappointed to be denied the chance, for whatever reason, to continue with the colourful way of life engendered at Goldsmith Building. It was a time to pause, look around and take stock of the situation. I was not now entirely certain that I wanted to return to the Temple, but at least, whilst waiting for Frank to contact me with any news, I could assess whether the magic of the place still held me, or whether there was any reasonable and viable alternative employment that I should consider.

Physically things had undoubtedly changed. The bombing had been more severe than I had recalled or imagined and although one could feel the obvious relief of all concerned that peace had been restored, chaos was the order of the day. Albeit cheerfully, everyone was aware that much had to be done before the pre-War tranquillity was re-established in the profession.

I strolled amidst the ruins of those buildings which had been badly hit and tried to recapture my earlier euphoria. I checked up on the destiny of some of my legal heroes, and was sorry to see that nearly all of the 'giants' had moved on to other pastures.

Sir William Jowitt's political leanings had produced an unusual pattern to his life. He had accepted the law officer's post of Solicitor-General from 1940 to 1942 in Churchill's Wartime all-party Government, notwithstanding the fact that he had held the more senior berth of Attorney General many years earlier, between 1929 and 1932 in the then Labour administration. In 1945 with the socialists again in power, he had been given the 'big one'. Attlee had appointed him Lord Chancellor, a post he was to hold for the six years leading up to the return of a Conservative government. When that occurred in 1951 it was rumoured that Jowitt so enjoyed the exalted level of legal attainment, that he offered his continued services in that role, despite the change of party, when Churchill was considering his new cabinet.

Norman Birkett had succumbed to the lure of a High Court appointment during the middle of the War, although as with most such appointments, he suffered a drastic drop in income. As a judge he displayed all his warmth and compassion, but it is the opinion of many that such a successful 'advocate' silk does not necessarily make a good judge – the temptation to be partisan is sometimes irresistible – but he must have endeared himself sufficiently to the Lord Chancellor because he was later one of the two British judges (the other being Mr. Justice Lawrence) sent to Nuremburg. [Here along with two each from the

U.S.A., U.S.S.R., and France, he and Lawrence sat in judgment of the Nazi war criminals. Ultimately, he was elevated to the Court of Appeal, where he remained until his retirement.

Sir Stafford Cripps left the Bar in 1940 to take up the important post of Ambassador to Russia during the period of dire uncertainty as to that country's involvement in the European War. In 1942, with the Communists ranged on our side. He returned to London as Lord Privy Seal and Leader of the House in the National Government. Churchill, later that year, moved him to the vital role of Minister of Aircraft Production, following Lord Beaverbrook's record-breaking efforts in that office. There he remained until the end of the War, when Attlee made him President of the Board of the Trade in his first Cabinet. In 1947 as a result of a re-shuffle he became Chancellor of the Exchequer, where he remained until 1950. He died in 1952.

The only one of the Big Four still in practice was Sir Patrick Hastings. Although he, too, had had political aspirations earlier on (he had been an M.P. from 1922 to 1926 and served as Attorney General for a short time in 1924), he played no part in an administrative role during the War. What he did do was to volunteer to join the RAF and took up balloon barrage duties in south London for a while. This enabled him to remain, at least partially, in practice throughout and it was nice to learn that his wizardry as a legal showman, was still available for all to see. He remained as such and was a most effective silk for a few more years before he also died in 1952.

Gilbert Beyfus had remained a force to be reckoned with in the front row throughout, earning a nickname of 'the Fox' until his death in 1960.

Sir Donald Somerville had continued to be Attorney General until 1945 when, for a short time he acted as Home Secretary. In 1946 he was made a High Court Judge and was soon elevated to the Court of Appeal. Finally, he became a Law Lord until his death in 1960.

St. John Field had never struck gold as a silk, although in 1945 he was appointed a County Court Judge and died four years later.

Richard O'Sullivan, the one responsible for my entry into the Temple, also failed to make an indelible mark as a K.C. He remained a Catholic speaker of colourful dimensions and was a central figure in the affairs of the St. Thomas More Society.

The one I was most interested in, of course, was the great VH! Valentine Holmes had made history in that, by invitation, he had stayed as Junior Treasury Counsel until almost the end of the War. As he was appointed to that post in 1935 he had exceeded the statutory period by at least three years and, as stated earlier, was totally disinterested in accepting the usual reward of a High Court judgeship. Instead (and at least this was contrary to his earlier intentions), he applied for, and almost automatically, was given his silk gown in April 1945 by the then Lord Chancellor. So that by 1946, when he was knighted for his exceptional services to the Treasury as their 'legal eagle', not surprisingly, he had already joined the ranks of the very successful K.C.s who emerged in the early post-War era

I was told by Frank that the reason he had changed his mind about joining the front row was that the heavy burden of paper work had finally got him down. As a silk he would still be required to advise in writing in a few cases, but he would be spared the enormous pressure of drafting endless pleadings and other documents which is the prerogative of the junior Bar. The last thing that VH would have wanted was the prestige or status of that higher level of the Bar, a sentiment which, with most other aspirants, had always been an overriding consideration. Notwithstanding, he was now even more to the forefront in causes celebres, especially in defamation cases (such as the Neville Laske libel action), in which, as with all his legal endeavours, he excelled.

Such was the scene at the common law Bar in mid-1946. As far as my pre-service Temple colleagues were concerned, I was saddened to hear that Edward had been killed on active service in the RAF soon after I had joined up. Most of the others including Ron Goldsmith and Ron Burley had returned intact and resumed where they had left off.

As my demobilisation leave was soon to end, I was required to report to Cardington for the few weeks which were to elapse before my discharge from the services. I had intended to use this period for a final analysis of my hopes and desires for the future, and to mull over what I had seen and heard on my recent visit to the Temple. My provisional view was that, if at all possible, I ought to try something else in the commercial field. My limited employment as a typist and general office assistant in Cairo at least ensured that the old skills, such as they were, had not become too rusty. However, just two days before leaving, I received an urgent note from Frank Connett to the effect that he wanted me to meet one of his many pals, Walter Butler, who I had not previously encountered and who was looking for a junior in his specialised Privy Council Chambers at No. 2 Paper Buildings, just around the corner.

Frank had apparently strongly recommended me, although I had had no experience in that rarefied field and urged me to return to the Temple at once. With nothing to lose and as time was short, I went up in the early evening so that he could introduce me. Typical of the times and of the people involved, the interview took place in a public house at about 6 o'clock and lasted about three pints. Frank had taken an active interest in the discussions and had insisted that if I took the job, he and I should remain on good terms in the future; a sentiment with which I was in full agreement. I immediately warmed to Walter Butler. Favourable terms having been offered I decided to give it a try, and the friendly get together culminated in handshakes all round.

It only remained for me to get demobilised and to collect my civilian suit which went with my discharge papers. Slightly more happy with events, I travelled to Cardington the next day. Effecting my departure from the RAF did not take long, and now having got some employment which appeared to be promising, I reported for duty with Wally (as he preferred to be called) and looked forward to the future. Although I nursed more than a pang of regret at not being able to continue working as before, I was now nevertheless eager to get back into the swing of the unique Temple.

It seemed a good move forward in all the circumstances. After the years away, I had to take a little time to adjust, but Wally Butler was such a friendly and engaging personality that I soon got used to the new environment and began to forget what might have been in Goldsmith Building.

From the start we got on well together and settled down as a team quite quickly. Although I was Wally's first junior, there was no third clerk as such. The only other occupant of the clerks room was our typist, Joyce, the daughter of the Temple fireman. She also managed the shop when Wally and I went off to court, usually four days a week.

This meant, of course, that I had to lug more books and papers mainly to and from the Privy Council, which is housed just inside Downing Street, off Whitehall. For this purpose we used cabs or occasionally the trams which then ran along the Embankment. Our chambers' practice was substantially involved with this elevated level of legal appeals. The Privy Council shares with the House of Lords the privilege of being the Highest Court in the realm, both being manned by Law Lords, the country's top judges.

The House of Lords' Appeals Board is the final court of appeal for all legal cases appertaining to the United Kingdom, whilst the Judicial Committee of the Privy Council is the ultimate forum for our overseas territories, including by agreement, some of the Commonwealth countries. Apart from civil matters, the Privy Council also possesses the ultimate jurisdiction in criminal cases from the colonies, where the death penalty for a convicted murderer was or is still in existence even though it has been abolished in the United Kingdom.

There is a macabre story of some years ago relating to an appeal from one of the colonies. Mr. John Huzan, Q.C., had been retained to appear before the Committee to represent a person, who had been found guilty of murder in his native land and had been sentenced to death. The convicted man naturally wanted to appeal to the highest authority.

The silk's programme at that time was such that he was not available for quite a few weeks to conduct the important hearing before their Lordships. Consequently, as it was a capital offence, the listing officer at the Privy Council agreed at the request of Huzan's clerk and with no objection from those representing the prosecution to a series of short postponements whenever a date had been proposed. Finally, two or three months later, the appeal was called on for hearing. Just as Mr. Huzan was about to rise to his feet to open the proceedings, the presiding Law Lord made a statement to the effect that information had just been received that unfortunately the appellant had in fact been executed a few days before. Notwithstanding, the offer was then made to hear the appeal, as a matter of determination of law, if no one disagreed; and the matter, therefore, was duly argued in the normal way. Ultimately the committee found that whilst it was to be regretted that the sentence had already been carried out, they nevertheless upheld the decision of the lower courts and confirmed the conviction.

It remains a point of hypothesis what they would have said or what would have happened if their Lordships had found in favour of the wretched appellant.

CHAPTER NINE
Now you see it – Now you don't

Our Chambers comprised two K.C.s – one, who was the head, sporting the intriguing title of Cuthbert Snowball Rewcastle, and the other, Samuel Khambatta, the youngest ever Indian Silk at the English Bar – he was about 38 years of age. The remainder were split between English and Indian juniors practising mainly in the Privy Council, but with a restricted amount of work in my old hunting ground, the Law Courts, across the Strand. Wally was only too pleased to leave me generally to manage anything requiring clerking there, while he dealt deftly, as only he could, with the specialised handling of the mainstream of work in the Higher Court.

It was soon apparent to me that he was an operator of remarkable qualities. If Adam was extreme as a pedantic and aloof, albeit unpopular clerk, and Frank was the best of the easy going and attractive kind, Wally portrayed yet another style and was by far the rarest of the types. He had the ability or prowess to manufacture work for his charges culled out of nothing – as if by magic.

Not having any household names like Gerald Gardiner or VH to give his chambers a swinging sign he had to start from scratch and promote the illusion. It is true that Dingle, the brother of Michael Foot, was a fairly successful member of his team and practised both in the Privy Council and the West Country within the area of influence of the Foots' father, the strong-minded Isaac. But his reputation was mainly political, he being one of the few Liberal devotees of that time. Later, having changed his allegiance to the Labour Party, Dingle Foot being M.P. for

Ipswich, and ultimately was appointed by Harold Wilson to the post of Solicitor General.

Two of Wally's many attributes were his enthusiasm and boundless energy. He was lean and wiry, and like many of his colleagues, drank fairly heavily, but, as with them, he was never under the influence or the worse for this particular pursuit. He possessed a most unusual fascination for women, although no one could describe him as a 'lady killer'. I think they wanted to mother him. He had a thin, boyish, almost anaemic face with large floppy ears.

Wally was happily married with no less than seven children and lived at Westcliff-on-Sea. He never seemed to rest or relax and went about his business with a remarkable fervour. He held no snobbish attitudes and had no false pride.

Above all, Wally enjoyed life very much and went out of his way to include me in his social as well as professional pursuits. This meant an invitation to join him and his contemporaries on almost every occasion he went drinking with them. It had become the practice anyway, on Friday evenings after work, for Senior and Junior Clerks to mix together for drinks in The Feathers, just off the Temple, in Tudor Street. This establishment was yet another where the law and the press overlapped.

Wally would use this drinking house as an alternative to El Vinos in his quest to remain on the warmest terms with so many of his legal friends and acquaintances. He was particularly anxious to be popular with all concerned, and as a result, develop work for his chambers' members.

He had, however, one unfortunate mode of behaviour – he was a most pronounced 'romancer' – he would say the first thing which came into his head, irrespective of the veracity of his statements. At times, even if the truth portrayed him in a more attractive light with whatever he was promulgating, he found it hard and sometimes impossible to resist 'gilding the lily'.

As his junior and often knowing that Wally was exaggerating, I found it difficult to admire him for this aspect of his otherwise engaging personality. Nevertheless his endeavours were fully productive. I had no intention of copying his manoeuvres which although ingenious, were sometimes dangerous. He never fully confided in me the secrets of his success but inevitably I learned something of his methods. It was a most intriguing exercise. Seeking to get on good terms with almost everyone within his horizon, he made a special point of befriending the lawyers and agents who came over from India and Ceylon to attend their appeals in the Privy Council.

Such people, staying for a few days only, were often alone in the great metropolis of London and Wally's invitations to dinner or lunch were doubly appreciated and made him very popular with all of them. They came from all classes and creeds and from all the different states of India (the split into the two nations of India and Pakistan had yet to take place). As the warmth of the association developed over the meal, Wally would say how grateful he would be if, on his return to his native land, his guest could keep him informed, perhaps by air letter, of any future appeals which appeared to be coming over from the Federal Court of the appropriate State. Just the name of the case would do and would be useful for Wally to look out for such matters in his general planning of the chambers' diary if he was fortunate enough to be instructed on either side.

The chances of being so instructed by normal means were fairly good, there being only about four sets which so specialised. His guests invariably promised to put Butler's name forward on their return, if at all possible, as well as supply the names by letter. Wally was not content, however, to leave it there. On receipt, sometime later, of the requested information he would proceed to telephone his closest contact, with whom he had developed a friendship, in the six or seven firms of London solicitors who were recognised as Privy Council agents. This would be, in some cases, one of the partners and in others, the legal executive then known as the 'managing clerk'. All had in common the fact that they were virtually in charge of the conduct if that firm received the retainer from India. One of their prime duties was to suggest to those instructing from abroad, which London barrister or barristers should be employed in the appeal over here.

Wally's call was to inform his friend that there was an appeal on its way over, called, say, 'Abdul Abass Singh versus the National Bank of Hyderabad' and that he, Wally, had 'strongly recommended' that that solicitor should be assigned. The recipient in thanking him, not unnaturally hinted that when the instructions were formally received, the choice of Counsel would be decided only after consultation with Wally.

This conversation would be repeated five or six more times with the other London agents, ultimately obtaining the same gratifying reactions. Thus, it will be seen that the chances of chambers being involved were increased considerably by this ploy. The instructions from India would come to one or other of the recognised firms in the normal course of events, anyway. It was even better than at first appreciated – two London agents would be contacted by those in India, one each side. So, two out of seven would report back to Wally eventually and Counsel would be duly designated.

It was like Russian roulette with Wally wondering which of his chickens would hatch. Once it was known which were the lucky ones, a tidying up job had to be done. This took the form of another call by Wally to the 'losers', informing them in a conciliatory way of his annoyance that his advice on choice of London agents had been ignored in India. This invariably resulted in a genuine acknowledgement of his efforts by those concerned with no deterioration of the existing rapport. Indeed, it could be argued that it was thereby improved.

Butler was not so successful, however, when it came to communicating all this with his barristers. Instead of a discreet silence (not exactly Wally's style) he would go separately and 'confidentially' from one to another, reporting that he had put that person's name forward to be selected in the appropriate case. Again, perhaps two would ultimately be rewarded, or even more if Silks were required. But members of chambers living in close communion with each other, unlike solicitors, would let slip over a morning coffee expedition to Grooms or an afternoon tea party to Twinings, their expectations as Wally had indicated.

That is strange! would be the reply from others. He told me that my name had been suggested. It was always amusing to hear the excuses which were put forward for these duplications when and if he was challenged. It was so unnecessary but typical of Wally's irrepressible enthusiasm for recognition.

There was one occasion which markedly illustrates the point: I was engaged in the clerks room one day, typing an urgent document for despatch (Joyce was away ill at the time and I had to deputise). Suddenly, we received a telephone message notifying us that a two- or three-day appeal in the High Court was imminent for listing the following day. This was bad news for the Counsel concerned, Mr. Phineas Quass, because he was on risk that another case, a civil trial, was also likely to be listed in the King's Bench Division. I primed Wally of the problem and suggested to him that, as the typing was required almost immediately, perhaps he would like to go across the road and try to avoid the clash. This he was loath to do, mainly I expect because he did not know quite how to go about it. It would, of course, have been balm to him if the cases concerned the Privy Council.

"Be a good chap, Tom – go over and sort it out" said Wally. "I'll make sure that there is no criticism of delay with the typing."

Phineas Quass occupied the room next to the clerks and always liked to have his door open, when not in conference, in order to hear what was going on. He was naturally most anxious not to be in two courts simultaneously the next day.

In the Law Courts a few minutes later, I checked firstly that the appeal, being the higher level, was definitely going to be listed on the morrow. That being so, I then proceeded to another part of the building, to see the Clerk of the Lists in charge of the civil trials. He was a kindly and helpful man called Boland and, having heard that our man was in the Court of Appeal the next day, he readily agreed to postpone the other case for a day or two if I kept him posted, especially as our opponent raised no objection. This simple exercise was in keeping with normal clerking procedure.

On returning to Paper Buildings, I reported the good news to Butler.

"Well done Tom" said he and immediately went into Phineas Quass's room via the open door to announce, within my hearing:

"Sir, I've just been over and seen the Court of Appeal people and ascertained that your case is definitely listed in their court tomorrow. This meant, of course, that I had to do something with your King's Bench case. I then went to see Townsend, the Clerk of the Lists, who happens, thank God, to be a very good friend of mine. I finally persuaded him to keep the other one out for a while, and under the Old Pals' Act, that is what he has promised to do.

"Thank you so much Walter," said Quass. "It's good that we have such friends at court, isn't it?"

With that Wally departed for his statutory lunchtime gin and tonic in The Feathers. As soon as he had gone, Phineas Quass, fully alive to the fact that the typewriter had not been clicking for a while and probably aware that Wally had remained throughout in the clerks room, came out and said to me: "Tom, will you tell Wally or shall I that his good friend Townsend retired as Clerk of the Lists over twelve months ago?"

Of course the members of chambers as well as the appropriate solicitors were not so gullible that they were fully taken in by Wally's quaint way of doing business. But at the end of the day they all appreciated that, by whatever unusual means, he mainly produced the goods. They also acknowledged that he was a most lively character and reliable friend in any crisis, who relished being involved. He was also very understanding and considerate to other people's feelings. He was a great morale booster and always looked on the bright side. Perhaps he could not have operated so effectively without his sense of 'romance'.

Another way in which Wally enhanced his influence generally came about when, whilst developing his social circle in El Vinos, he made the acquaintance of and soon became friends with the 'Stroller' of *The Evening News*, one of three evening papers circulating at the time. The Stroller was the theatre critic for *The News* and was responsible for a short column of about three paragraphs each day. This included reviews of first nights, gossips about producers, sponsors, actors and actresses generally and any other snippets which might interest his readers. But he often found it difficult to maintain a fresh and literal flow, relating to the theatre fraternity every evening.

Wally came to his rescue now and again by supplying information regarding the legal world. This might be any item of newsworthiness but mainly would be in the nature of disclosing the names of K.C.s who were rumoured to have been retained in certain cases soon to be heard in the Privy Council, the Law Courts, or even the Old Bailey.

In those days, just after the War, there were many fashionable civil cases, mainly libel and slander and breach of promise. Also murder trials were few and far between because of the death penalty, and were reported by the media much more fully than today. The general public therefore took more notice and the Stroller's column was, occasionally with Wally's help, made more topical and interesting to his readers. The critic reciprocated by passing on complimentary tickets for many of the shows then running in the West End, including once in a while, first nights. These 'freemans' would be given by Wally to, amongst others, his Privy Council solicitor friends and overseas visitors, thus promoting his reputation further in that direction. All in all, he had established himself as a person of great influence and occupied a central position in many areas of activity, particularly in anything to do with the Privy Council.

Even Lord Gavin Simmonds, who had been Lord Chancellor and who was the senior Law Lord presiding over most of the Indian appeals for some years after the War, regarded Wally Butler as a friend and confidante. He consulted him when his son, also named Gavin, was called to the Bar, and, as a result, the young Simmonds entered Wally's Chambers for pupillage and later as a tenant. It is worth noting that, when one or two of our Indian agents arrived for their appeals and realised that the son of the presiding judge was in Wally's chambers the offspring was suddenly the recipient of a very junior brief to sit as an additional member of the legal team at the hearing. The fee offered was not very big, but his appearance before his father was, quite erroneously, thought by the Indians to be an inducement for the clients. Such an attempt would, if anything, have the adverse effect but, of course, in the high echelons of the British legal system it was a total waste of time. It was really quite laughable, although the young counsel concerned did not mind – nor did Walter!

Butler's quest for excitement resulted in him arranging, through one of his many solicitor friends, a no-limit account with a firm of book-makers in Pinner, Middlesex. It soon became apparent to me that he was a very heavy, if not compulsive gambler. Hardly a day would go by without a number of telephone calls to the company to enquire the odds on an imminent race, followed by the wagering of a £1 or two on his chosen nag. Ten minutes later there would be another call to ascertain the winner.

In the course of only a few weeks Wally's many pals around the Temple discovered that by ringing chambers they could get a bet on, having been encouraged to do so by the irrepressible Wally as part of his popularity drive.

It soon fell to my lot to be the one who effected all the wagers and to deal with the arithmetic (plus or minus) when the statement came in at the end of the week. This invariably meant a great deal of chasing people for their losses. It was a job I did not enjoy very much but difficult to refuse to do, as I had become on good terms with most of the clerks who rang through.

Also a few members of chambers, including the young Gavin Simmons, started to have a 'flutter' from time to time. Although we managed to continue to do our clerking somehow, the office did, occa-sionally, have the look of a part-time betting shop about it.

After a while the pressure of business with the bookmakers mounted considerably, culminating into a saturation situation during the Derby week of that particular year. It was then that I burnt my fingers rather badly. The great race was run on a Saturday in those days. I went into chambers in the morning to telephone about 150 bets which had accumulated throughout the week by all concerned. These ranged from a maximum of about £10 from the heavies down to the odd shilling or so as the annual investment chosen by the spouses or junior office staff. In all the list ran into about six or seven foolscap sheets.

I was just about to start the long laborious task when one of my old

RAF buddies, Les Whiting, called into the clerks room to inveigle me out for a lunchtime drink and sandwich prior to going off to the Oval to watch Surrey do battle at cricket in the afternoon. When he saw the size of the number of bets involved, which obviously would take quite a while to transmit, he suggested that we should have a go at acting as bookmakers ourselves. In this way, we could save a bit of time and, hopefully, show a joint profit. After a brief study of the sheets we decided to pass through only the twenty or so bigger bets and take our chance on the scores of smaller wagers, which were anything from one to ten shillings, with perhaps an odd £1 or two. We came to the conclusion that it could not be disastrous because of the modest stakes and the fairly wide choice of horses selected. Having agreed that and put it into practice, we went off on our social exploits, looking forward eagerly to the fruits of great enterprise.

Alas, it was the year My Love won the Derby at very generous odds, and on a closer look at the list, almost everyone had added a little bob each way on the winner 'for the wife' or for the girl in the office. In all it cost us both about £15 (about two weeks' wages). Ironically, had we stood the lot, we would have shown a profit. It was the first and definitely the last occasion I was to be tempted in that way.

Sometime later Wally was good enough to persuade his bookmaker to recognise my efforts, in acting as a handler of quite a bit of their business (the money flow seemed to go one way only), by giving me 3d in the £1 commission. This was great news, but inevitably, I was prone to have a few flutters myself (I'm only playing with their money anyway I comforted myself by saying). As my luck was not very good there was little joy as a result.

We were not the only clerks' room which developed a diversionary pursuit. Around the corner in Temple Gardens the head, Mr. Gilbert Pauli K.C., was responsible for giving his two clerks, Basil and Norman, a block of shares one year as a Christmas present. It was, apparently, a sizeable amount, and he accompanied it with good advice as to the manipulation of buying and selling on the Stock Exchange. In time, other members of that set of chambers joined with their clerks in doing business over the telephone. If our operation was similar to a small-time bookmaker's office, their additional afternoon activities took on the shape of a stockbroker's office. It was rumoured that, in pooling their assets and know-how, they, unlike us, all did very well out of their efforts. Fortunately we had in common the ability to operate as a busy set of chambers at the same time.

Yet another set took on a non-legal interest. Mr. Edward Tyrell, the head, was an inventor as well as a barrister and was paid very handsome royalties for producing these inventions. His two clerks spent time during office hours as well as at their homes, trying to emulate their boss in making our lives easier with similar revelations. The senior clerk, it is claimed, got close to solving the problem of coastal flooding caused by lashing seas during heavy storms. The installations required were apparently quite workable but far too costly.

In mid-1947, along with Les Whiting, I joined the Catholic tennis club in Ilford's Valentine's Park. Social life in Bow was then almost non-existent – even the tin hut next to the church in Bow Road, once the centre of our teenage life, had been destroyed by enemy action. The only flicker of joy was that the Conservative Club, not far away, surprisingly flourished despite being in the heart of the Labour stronghold of Poplar.

My father had joined this club during the War and enjoyed the amenities which included snooker and various gambling games of cards, such as Brag and Poker. On my return, following our exchange of letters, he and I became very close and it was a matter of only a moment before I too had become a member. I soon learnt to chalk a cue and 'up the ante'. Unfortunately no one played Bridge and there were no tennis clubs nearby. I had to go the four or five miles to find Bridge playing tennis enthusiasts. So I alternated between the green baize and gambling midweek and the more temperate tennis and Bridge at weekends. The latter offered much more in the sense of mixing with my own age group and the sports club, being open to both sexes, became an obvious place for consorting. A number of engagements and marriages ensued over a period and it was there that I met my wife, Angela.

Although quite resolutely no Bridge player, she was no mean

performer with a racquet. In time, after we had become engaged, we spent quite a few evenings in London enjoying the theatre. We were encouraged to do so by my enthusiastic senior clerk plying us with some of the Stroller's complimentary tickets. There was a period when we could boast that we had seen every worthwhile show in the West End – if we had no free admissions we queued up for the balconies. We also mixed with Wally on many of his tireless social activities in town.

It was an exciting and happy period of my life, but I was beginning to feel, very slowly at first, that the Privy Council did not offer an all-embracing area for barrister clerking. At best it sat in two courts only and as rumours began to creep in that India, at the point of obtaining independence, would elect to give up its option to use the final Court of Appeal in London, unlike some other Commonwealth countries, most of the work there would cease.

Also, as we planned to get married, it would be nice if I could improve my lot, if possible, by becoming a senior clerk preferably back in the common law field of the Law Courts. But that is easier said than done. It is usually a case of waiting to fill 'dead men's shoes' and, even if I had been content to stay with Wally, it was fairly certain that he had many years of vibrant professional life left in him anyway. It was also likely that the overall success of chambers would be curtailed, at least in the short term, by the loss of the Indian work. It would be difficult to expect any substantial increase in salary, as a result.

Keeping him fully informed of my hopes and aspirations and with his every blessing, I decided to see what might be on offer.

Final note:

Sadly, Frank (aka Tom) never wrote any more of his story before he passed away. I think you will agree it is a fascinating story and I'm so pleased it has finally been published. Thank you once again to Frank's wife and family for allowing me to include this in my story.

It also reminds me to say that if someone has a story to tell, they should get it written down as soon as they can and share it with their families. I decided to write my story because of the number of times I've been told by friends: "When I retire, I'll write my story". Don't wait, start writing.

Frank (aka Tom) obviously continued to work as a Barristers' Clerk in the Temple for many years as meeting Tom was where my personal story started.

Stephen Ward

If you have a funny story about life in the legal profession, please do send it onto me using ward@clerksroom.com so it can be considered for the next volume of this book, if there is ever another book of tales from the Clerksroom.

Frank in the Air Force

Frank at his desk

Frank with the Q.C.'s

Frank, his wife and son, outside 2 Crown Office Row, Temple.

Lightning Source UK Ltd.
Milton Keynes UK
UKHW041043221121
394391UK00001B/129